Y0-CBI-447

DONALD J. HURZELER

WAY UP

HOW *to* KEEP YOUR CAREER
MOVING *in the* RIGHT DIRECTION

GREENLEAF
BOOK GROUP PRESS

Published by Greenleaf Book Group Press
Austin, Texas
www.gbgpress.com

Distributed by Greenleaf Book Group LLC

For ordering information or special discounts for bulk purchases, please contact Greenleaf Book Group LLC at PO Box 91869, Austin, TX, 78709, 512.891.6100.

Design and composition by Greenleaf Book Group LLC and Alex Head
Cover design by Greenleaf Book Group LLC

Publisher's Cataloging-In-Publication Data
Hurzeler, Donald J.
    The way up : how to keep your career moving in the right direction / Donald J. Hurzeler. -- 1st ed.
    p. ; cm.
    Includes bibliographical references.
    ISBN: 978-1-60832-087-5
    1. Career development. 2. Vocational guidance. 3. Success in business. I. Title.
HF5381 .H87 2011
650.14   2010935071

Part of the Tree Neutral® program, which offsets the number of trees consumed in the production and printing of this book by taking proactive steps, such as planting trees in direct proportion to the number of trees used: www.treeneutral.com

Printed in the United States of America on acid-free paper

10 11 12 13 14 15   10 9 8 7 6 5 4 3 2 1

First Edition

DEDICATION

This book is dedicated to my wife, Linda. She lets me write books when we could be out snorkeling.

From the first moment I met Linda, I have been deeply in love. She lights up a room with her beauty. She lights up my life with her care and companionship. And she can stare down a quite dangerous shark without ever blinking—my kind of woman.

Linda, I love you completely. Let's see if we can continue to find adventures that will keep us smiling for the rest of our lives.

—Don

THE WAY UP: HOW TO KEEP YOUR CAREER MOVING IN THE RIGHT DIRECTION

Career strategies for
- Recent high school and college graduates just starting their careers.

- Men and women joining the workforce after serving in the armed forces (and thank you for that service).

- Men and women who chose to stay at home to raise the kids and are now embarking on their own careers (and thank you for that service).

- Men and women who are in mid-career and who wish to be more successful.

This quick read will
- Help you get your career off to a great start.

- Show you ways to increase your options for success.

- Give you strategies for dealing with the ups and downs of a successful career.

- Teach you business secrets that will put you ahead of your competition.

CONTENTS

INTRODUCTION

"Don't be afraid of the space between your dreams and reality.
If you can dream it, you can make it so."
—Belva Davis

Not everyone strives to be a success, but apparently you do. I would be honored to help you on your way.

The basic theme of this book is that you can make some fairly simple choices that will put you head and shoulders above most of your competition. If you put these ideas into action and stay committed to them over a lifetime, good things will happen. Success will happen.

Everyone defines success differently. I define success as a feeling of accomplishment, lots of happiness to go alongside the difficulties we all face in both the workplace and at home, the financial rewards that come from being a valued employee, and the satisfaction of reaching one or more of the grand goals for your life. If that sounds about right to you, I think you are going to find this book useful.

I do not pretend to have all the answers, nor do I pretend to be the most successful person in the world. However, I've had forty years of experience in Corporate America, and my career has met every one of the criteria for success that I described in the preceding paragraph.

In my career, I have soared high, been kicked to the curb, got back up, and moved on ahead. I never tried to win every time. However, I was—and still am—determined to win everything in the end.

If you are scared at the prospect of competing in your new career or afraid/concerned/depressed because you are in mid-career and have not yet been successful, welcome to the club. Careers are not easy. I'm offering you help. You *can* do this; you *can* compete, and you *can* win.

So let's get started.

PART ONE

PROVE YOUR VALUE

You will soon learn that this book was not written by a brain surgeon. In fact, when I showed the draft of this book to a couple of my successful friends, both said they know all this stuff, that they should have written this book.

Happily for me, they were too busy and never found the time to get these ideas down on paper. I did. (As you read the book, please imagine that those much smarter and more successful people actually wrote it.)

Careers are part 100-meter dash and part marathon. You absolutely need to get off to a great start (or a great restart), and you also will need plans to help you run the marathon part of your career-long race. We will hit on the sprint portion of your career in Part One of the book. Later we will work on your long-run success.

Remember the old saying about first impressions, that you get only one chance to make a first impression? This first part of the book is about making great first impressions. This part gets you off and running in a way that *will* be noticed. A first impression enables you to start distinguishing yourself in the workplace. This is when you first begin to look like the winner you are working to be.

My first job was with a very large company. The first day at work I noticed hundreds of gray desks all lined up in rows. Each desk had a person sitting behind it. As I got to know these people, I found them to be as smart as or smarter than me. They all seemed like winners. (Almost all of them. There was this one guy who wore a hat at his desk, had a big beer belly, and wore a bow tie.) Along the front wall of the building were all these glassed-in offices—Executive Row.

Looking at all these employees, I thought, "How am I ever going to move ahead of the herd of people at those desks and all those entrenched executives who already have the world by the tail? How will I compete?"

It is a good time to ask yourself the same thing: How do I plan to compete? Only you can answer that question. But answer it you must. You need to find that one thing that sets you apart from everyone else, that makes you unique and valuable. The world is full of *average*. *Good* is in ample supply. *Unique*, now that's valuable.

What will you do that will make you unique and valuable? I say unique *and* valuable because becoming the only known cannibal at work would make you unique, but it wouldn't make you valuable.

You will be unique and valuable if you become

- *The* subject matter expert, the person who knows more about and has had more experience with a specific subject than anyone else in the world.

- *The* acknowledged expert on turning around unprofitable companies.

- *The* person companies turns to when they need to cut expenses.

- *The* best communicator in times of change.

- *The* best leader for companies in a growth mode.

- *The* best sales person.

I italicized *The* because I want to emphasize that unique means the one and only. It's very difficult to become *the* anything. However, there is usually room for more than one at the top, so I always imagine that unique means being somewhere in the top 1 percent. It's a very exclusive club you will need to join if you want to enjoy great success.

Part One will not select that unique thing for you. That will be up to you. It will get you off to a great start so that when you do begin to define your unique place in the business, your reputation will propel you to the top. Unique sometimes takes years to develop. The habits described in Part One will pay dividends starting today. As I said, this is the sprint part of the book.

On your marks . . .

CHAPTER ONE

LET'S START EASY: SHOW UP ON TIME, AND GOOD THINGS HAPPEN.

"You will find the key to success under the alarm clock."
—Benjamin Franklin

THE CASE FOR SHOWING UP TO WORK ON TIME, EVERY TIME

Early in my career I earned an educational distinction that caught the eye of the chairman of the board of a very large local company. He invited me, and about twenty others who also had earned the distinction, to have lunch with him and his board of directors in the board dining room of their beautiful home office. This was a company I thought I might want to work for at some point, so I jumped at the opportunity to attend the lunch.

On the day of the event, I was traveling. As the plane carried me from Reno to Las Vegas to Orange County, California, it became clear that I was going to be late for the lunch. This was in the days before the cell phone (yes, there were days before the cell phone), and I had no way to notify the chairman of my situation. I was horrified.

When the plane finally landed, I figured that if I drove at a semi-safe speed of something like ninety miles per hour, I could get to the luncheon only fifteen minutes late. I put the pedal to the medal and careened across Orange County. When I arrived, I was directed to the board dining room. The door was closed—and locked. Through the door I could hear people talking and the sounds of lunch being served. Oh, this was going to be awful. I gave serious consideration to turning away and just leaving.

Somehow I got up the nerve to knock on the door. As soon as I knocked, the whole room fell silent. Damn! This *was* going to be embarrassing. I heard someone heading toward the door and prepared myself for one of life's difficult moments. When the door opened I could see several tables of people. All of them had stopped eating so they could have a good look at me. One of them, a tall gentleman I recognized as the chairman, stood up. He asked if he could help me.

I said, "I am embarrassed to say that I am fifteen minutes late for the educational recognition luncheon."

The chairman smiled and looked around the room. He said, "Son, don't worry about a thing. You are actually *a week and fifteen minutes late for that meeting.* The luncheon was last week. What you have arrived late for this week is our board of directors meeting. Would you care to join us for lunch?"

At that point everyone in the room burst into laughter. The chairman tried to settle them down. When the laughter stopped he said, "I'm sorry, I missed your name."

I said, "Well, thank God for that."

More laughter followed as I fled to my car.

Showing up on time seems to be so easy. You certainly don't need to read a book to figure out that it's a good idea to be punctual.

Here is the problem: Many people, maybe even you, show up *kind of* on time. Despite the story I just told (which is absolutely true), I am here to tell you that much of the success I had early in my career started with my getting to the office on time, every time, come hell or high water.

The three or four times I was late during my forty-year career remain major embarrassments to me to this day.

So what is the big deal about showing up on time? Who cares if you're occasionally late? I mean, there are lots of legitimate excuses for being late: traffic problems, public transportation delays, kids getting sick. In fact, who cares if you arrive late when you intend to stay late tonight to make up for it? Who cares? I care. And your boss might be someone like me.

In the course of a career you are going to run into all kinds of bosses. Each one will have some quirk that you need to adjust to in order to be successful. Unfortunately, some bosses never will come right out and tell you about their quirks or pet peeves. They will just quietly pass over you when the time comes for promotions and bonuses. You may never even find out why.

The easiest way to get off to a great start in your new career is to just show up on time all the time. Be known for it. Become someone the boss can count on to be in the office or at the desk right at starting time. You may be the only one there. If so, then your punctuality helps distinguish you from your competition.

Showing up on time is more important than you think. Let me add another cautionary tale about a friend of mine who would be a superstar, except that she always arrives late to the office.

This young lady has it all. She is smart. She works hard and works long hours. She has a great personality. People love her. Heck, I love her.

Unfortunately, I think she believes that arriving late all the time lends her an air of mystery. I say "I think" because I have absolutely no idea why she does this day after day. And here is the fallout: People feel disrespected by her. They no longer trust her. Her excuses are considered laughable. If she is going to lie to her teammates about why she is late, what else is she saying that isn't true? They make fun of her behind her back. They also say things like, "I busted my butt to get here on time, and now I have to wait around for her to show up. It really pisses me off."

I'm not sure this woman has ever run into a boss who really cares whether people are on time. I do know that her boss's boss noticed her constant tardiness, and it cost her big time. In fact, it cost her at least one promotion. And it will continue to cost her.

Why take a chance on something as easy as just showing up on time?

So here is my first recommendation to anyone who is just starting or restarting his or her career with the absolute intention of becoming very successful at work: *show up on time every time.*

SHOW UP AT WORK WITH A GREAT ATTITUDE

Let me add in a couple other recommendations that will cost you nothing, are easy to do, and will catch the attention of your superiors at work and get you off to a great start.

Show up each day with a great attitude. There are whole books written on this subject, and I don't want to sound like the motivational speaker who lives in the trailer down by the river. However, people who show up on time each day and who have a great attitude toward work are in short supply.

Having a great attitude means that you support the program at work. You are easy to work with and to be around. Your boss doesn't have to worry about what you are saying behind his or her back. It means you will work hard for your own success and for the success of others and the team.

"It's all about presenting a trustworthy body who bleeds the corporate colors when wounded, who stands for something worth spending a lifetime defining and defending at all costs." My editor, Bob Gorman, wrote that to me in an e-mail, and I could not have said it better. Thanks, Bob.

Here comes a really wild segue, but hang in there with me.

I understand the purpose and need for unions. (See, I told you it was a wild segue.) I respect the gains they have helped make for their members. However, I have also noted what I call a "union attitude" from many union members—many but certainly not all. The attitude includes sentiments such as these:

"Management sucks."

"The company is trying to screw us again."

"I'm not paid to do that work."

"I'll show them that they can't mess with me; I'm calling in sick today."

"All that change they just told us about is designed to hurt us. I don't trust them. I will never support the change."

"Some things will never change, so I am not even going to try to help them bring about their latest nutty idea to improve the situation; I give up."

"Did you hear the latest rumor about how much money that management is preparing to pay themselves?"

If you are going to have a career as an hourly worker protected by a union, well, God bless you. America needs you. You are underappreciated, and I am sorry that is often the case. Thanks for taking on difficult jobs and doing them to the best of your ability. I hope that you have never made any of the preceding statements, but I will bet you have heard some of them from coworkers. These attitudes benefit no one.

A good attitude at work includes:

- Supporting management through thick and thin. If cut at work, bleed the company's blood. Be loyal to the company paying you the check. Understand and support the company vision and live it everyday.

- Embracing change. Businesses change all the time.

You are in for a career of change. Get accustomed to it. Learn how to support it. Look for the opportunities that exist in times of change. Change has to be your friend, not your enemy. All of my best opportunities at work have come during times of change. Yours will too.

• Being optimistic. "We can do it" is more than a slogan; it is a way of life. If you think you can do it, you can.

There's no need to be overly optimistic. If they fire 500 people in your office, put the building up for sale, and take away your company car, you may need to temporarily abandon your optimism. Once you have worked your way back into something that looks viable, rekindle that optimism and bring it to work every day.

Too many people abandon optimism at the first sign of trouble. You will have many challenges during a long career. Hold on to your optimism as long as you can. Lose it only when you have the facts on which you can base your loss of enthusiasm. For example, if the owner of the business you worked for hanged himself and left a note apologizing for his gambling away the pension fund that would be a legitimate reason to become negative.

• Being willing to get the ox out of the ditch. This means that you will do whatever needs to be done when times are tough. As long as it is ethical, jump in the ditch and pitch in to save the company. There are no jobs that are "beneath" you. Do whatever is needed now.

I once hired a guy who had an MBA from Notre Dame. On his first day at work we needed to get copies of reports run for the quarterly meeting with the CEO. When I asked him to run a bunch of copies he said, and I quote, "You mean, I went to school and got my MBA so I could come here and run a copy machine?"

"Yup," I told him. "It's what's needs to be done right now. Careful now. Don't get any of that toner on your new suit."

Years ago one of the divisions of Motorola decided everyone would work six days a week for five days' pay. The division made this decision because the business otherwise would fail. I admire that kind of attitude.

- Being a good teammate. That doesn't mean you can't be tough when you need to be or that you have to put aside all hopes of individual recognition. It means that you will have more success if you are known as a good teammate than you will if no one ever wants you on his or her team. Good teammates hold themselves accountable for delivering on their promises to the team. They also hold their teammates accountable for delivering on the promises they make.

If you are not capable of being a good team player, you need to seriously consider a job that allows you to work alone, something outside of Corporate America. Nearly everyone works on teams in today's corporate workplace.

• Bringing energy to the office. I was born plugged into a wall socket. I have much more energy than I do good sense. Not everyone is like me. I understand that everyone has his or her own level of energy. I also understand that many people don't understand or trust my level of energy. I am sure that if you mope around the office and look like you are about a minute away from falling asleep while I am talking, it is not going to go well for you. Offices need energy to run. They need your energy. Find a way to get charged up and stay charged up at work. You may have to fake it a bit at first, but once you see the good results, it will become part of who you are.

What does it mean to have energy in the office?

You speak up in meetings.

You lean forward and face people when they are talking to you.

You are the first to volunteer.

You go out of your way to help your team complete the task.

DO WHAT YOU LOVE AND SHOW THE LOVE

Show that you are having fun at work. Most of the time you will be having fun. Let others know it with a smile. The workplace is filled with people with blank stares. Don't be one. Most people like people who smile and seem to be enjoying themselves. A few won't trust you. They will be suspicious. As Ricky Nelson once sang, "You can't please everyone." Keep smiling. I loved working in Corporate America, and it was fun. I'm smiling just thinking about it.

By the way, if you really are not having fun at work then *quit*. If work is not fun, you will run out of internal resources to keep you running long and hard for the level of success you desire. Work will wear you out. There are plenty of other jobs out there. Go get one that you enjoy. *Life is too short to be unhappy at work.*

That is actually the best advice I could ever give anyone. *Do what you love and let the world know you love it.*

MAKE YOUR WISH INTO A COMMITMENT

One last thing: Are you wishing for success, or are you willing to make a commitment to be successful? If you are just wishing, stop reading. This book isn't for you. If you are making a commitment to be successful, make it a signed-in-blood commitment and remember the words of my little friend:

> *"If you start to take Vienna, take Vienna."*
> —Napoleon Bonaparte

CHAPTER TWO

THIS PART'S A LITTLE HARDER: DO WHAT YOU SAY YOU WILL DO, ON TIME, EVERY TIME.

"You can't build a reputation on what you are going to do."
—Henry Ford

IT IS AS SIMPLE AS KEEPING YOUR WORD

There is nothing more valuable to a boss than a person who does what he or she agrees to do. That person can be trusted, allowing the boss to sleep better at night and to feel confident when speaking with his or her own boss. Someone who does what they say they will do—on time, every time—is a very rare and wonderful asset.

I have had a lifelong tendency to take on every possible job assignment or outside opportunity that comes my way. I am a high-energy worker. If it takes weekends and evenings to get the job done, count me in. I want to do my part and more. It is part of how I compete. I want to be the most valuable person on the team.

However, I found out the hard way that this strategy can wear you out and cause you to derail. There have been times in my life when I took on too much. I delivered on more than one person should be able to, yet I failed to deliver on everything I said I would do. I worked my butt off and made some people very happy, but I also made some people unhappy because I couldn't get their work done on time. As Tupac Shakur said in one of his songs, to work hard and disappoint, "That's no good for nobody."

IT IS GOOD TO VOLUNTEER AND HORRIBLE TO OVERCOMMIT

I have a couple of thoughts concerning this point. First, I favor taking on more than your fair share of work. It makes you more valuable than your competition. It's how you gain experience quicker than the next person. I think it is a good career strategy.

I also think it is good to take on work or leadership roles outside the workplace. I'm talking about being involved in Rotary, the United Way, or your place of worship, coaching Little League, or taking an industry position for professionals in your industry. The exposure helps you network. It builds skills that you may not be developing at work. It gives you experience and confidence that will help you at work.

However, when you add the extra work in the workplace to the extra work outside the workplace, things start to become difficult. You are making commitments and promises in two different directions. Those commitments may overlap in a mutually exclusive way. It's tricky business.

To be crystal clear, if you really want to be successful at work, you must not endanger your ability to deliver—every time—on your at-work promises. This is advice coming from someone who has famously overcommitted both at work and outside of work. Learn from me: You are better off focusing on one huge goal than on two or more.

One of the real highlights of my life was becoming the president of the Chartered Property Casualty Underwriters Society. This is an international organization of more than 25,000 insurance professionals who have earned the CPCU designation. I love the men and women of this organization. I am thankful to have served as their president.

At the same time that I was stepping into the leadership roles that would take me to the presidency of that organization, I was CEO of a sizable business. And just to make things a little more exciting, I was diagnosed with cancer. I didn't expect or want this to all happen at once (of course, I didn't want the cancer thing to happen at all), but it did.

Net result: I nearly killed myself trying to make everything work. I scheduled radiation treatments for seven in the morning so I could be at work by eight. I never missed a minute of work, although there were days when I was so worn out I was pretty useless in the office.

An aside on this last point: During the time of my radiation treatments I tried to get out of the office at an early hour, like 5:00 p.m. One afternoon I got caught up in something and when I finally realized what time it was, it was nearly seven in the evening. I drove home with my head out the window to stay awake (an exceedingly stupid thing to do; I should have called a car service). When I got home, I guess I pulled into the garage, turned off the car (thank God), and immediately fell asleep, with my forehead against the hub of the steering wheel. My wife did not hear me drive into the garage. When I awoke two hours later, I staggered into the house and found my wife in a panic. She had been looking for me for two hours. And now I was standing before her, with a Mercedes-Benz symbol embossed on my forehead. Not my brightest moment, although we smile about now. My work did suffer. I was too close to the situation to know the truth. But I do know this: My boss didn't think that I could do all three things. He probably had better sense than I did. He took me out of the CEO job and gave me something else to do that was a better fit for my situation. I didn't like it, but it may have saved my life.

Back on point: My outside commitment started small, but it built up to a point where the work absolutely conflicted with the job that paid me real money. Be very careful with your commitments. They can lead you into impossible situations. And if you do take on huge commitments outside of the workplace, be prepared to pay the price. I was prepared. I'm happy I took on the outside commitment. It didn't help my real work career at all, and since I was nearly sixty years old at that time, that was OK with me. But it wouldn't have been acceptable to me when I was in my forties.

Be careful about overcommitting. If you want huge success at work, put 98 percent of your efforts there. Use the other 2 percent to help others. You will have many more chances to give back to society, or your industry, after your success is assured.

Do what you say you will do each and every time and on time, and you will be a superstar at work.

"Responsible persons are mature persons who have taken charge of themselves and their conduct, who own their actions and own up to them, who answer for them."
—William J. Bennett

CHAPTER THREE

LEARN TO LISTEN.

"Listen. Do you want to know a secret?"
—The Beatles

OK, I know the Beatles were not singing about business skills. Nevertheless, they hit on one of the biggest secrets in business: Listening is much harder than speaking, and much more important.

YOUR LISTENING SKILLS CAN MAKE OR BREAK YOU

I worked with a lot of alpha males and females over the years. These are people who are all charged up on coffee, life, and their own egos—people just like me. We are not great listeners. In fact, most of us are rotten listeners.

I once had a terrific boss who, for the sake of the book, I will call Frank Patalano. That will work out just fine, because that was his actual name. Frank was one of the best bosses I've ever encountered. He was the strongest of the alpha males, hardworking, decisive, smart as hell, and driven to win. Frank could make the earth shake and people shake in their boots. If you wanted something done, you went and saw Frank.

However, Frank was not the world's best listener. He was so bad that he needed to be trained to listen properly. His problem was that he felt that every person speaking to him wanted his idea on how to solve a situation. Heck, some of us just wanted to tell him what we were already doing to solve a problem. Others of us just wanted to vent. A few of us were looking for a sympathetic shoulder to cry on. Frank would have none of that. We all got the same treatment. Frank would interrupt us as we were speaking, outline exactly how the problem was to be solved, yell at us for a while, and then send us packing. Like I said, he was not the world's best listener.

In an effort to improve the commitment and the communication skills of his team, Frank sent all of us, himself included, to get some training, from Loretta Malandro, PhD, of Malandro Communication Inc.

The training was life changing for some of us and especially so for Frank. He learned on the first day that he was part of the problem with our team. He learned that a major part of his problem was that he did not know how to listen effectively. To be fair, the rest of us also were pretty screwed up. We all had much to learn.

I will leave the techniques that Loretta and her team use to teach these skills to Loretta and her team. I highly recommend their services. You will find their contact information in the back of this book. What I will tell you is we learned that there are different ways to listen.

Many of us are not really listening. We are "already listening," a term I had encountered years before during some leadership training conducted by a group called DiBianca-Berkman. Already listening is very real for me. I do it all the time. I am getting better at stopping myself from doing it. I'm kind of like an alcoholic in recovery: I'm working on it one day at a time. We already-listening people do *not* listen to you. We can hardly wait for you to stop talking. In fact, we will probably interrupt you. Time is precious, and we knew exactly what needed to be done the second you opened your mouth. We were *already listening* to our own thoughts on how to solve your problem. When explained like that, already listening doesn't sound like an effective way to listen, does it? It is not.

Many of us, especially those with lots of experience and lots of confidence in our capabilities—people like Frank and me—had another listening fault. We thought you wanted us to solve your problems for you. We listened just long enough to know what to tell you to do, and then we were pretty much finished with the conversation. Again, that's not optimal listening.

Oh, there's more. Lots of people I know listen with the intention of finding a way to kill any of the ideas suggested by the speaker. They actually listen intensely, looking carefully for the crack in the logic so they can throw a spanner in the works (you might have to look up that reference and in doing so could find an excellent Rod Stewart album). These people are the killers of dreams and the assassins of innovation. They are legion in this world.

So here's what Frank and I learned from the Malandro

team: People enter into conversations for a number of reasons. Some want to complain, others to inform, brag, gain sympathy, float possible solutions, spark idea generation in partnership with the listener, build a relationship, get the listener to mentor the speaker or, in some cases, get the listener to actually take over the problem and solve it. There are lots of types of conversations and lots of ways the speaker wants the listener to listen. With Frank and me it was kind of one-size-fits-all. You talked, we listened to ourselves, and at the first opportunity we solved your problem, whether you wanted it solved or not.

Learn to listen properly. It may be as simple as asking the speakers how they want you to listen. When they look at you like you are crazy, just tell them what you mean. "Do you want me listen for possibilities? Are you here so I can help you solve a problem? Or do you just want to pass along some information? How do you want me to listen?"

I know that the scenario I just gave you sounds awkward. It is. So you need to find a way to make this strategy work for you. Give it some thought. And assume that you don't always know exactly how the speaker wants you to listen. If you can learn to listen effectively to those who wish to speak with you, you will become a very valuable person at work. You will learn the secrets—not the rumors or the nasty stuff—but the secrets of how people think. You will also help them to help you and the rest of the team win the day.

Let's move on to some other listening problems.

Have you ever noticed that people love to complain? Sure

you have. If you use your good listening skills to constantly let people tell you how bad it is for them, you are enabling them to be the victims they so dearly want to be. In fact, they may even wear down your good attitude and win you over to their black ring of Hell. This ring is called "resignation" (thanks again to Loretta Malandro and her team for this designation).

UNDERSTAND THE DARK POWER OF RESIGNATION

Resignation is all about being a victim. Have you ever heard any statements like these:

"Those stupid managers of our company are running us off the cliff."

"My first boss screwed me on a raise twenty years ago, and I have not trusted any boss since then."

"Women get all the good jobs here. Why even try to get promoted?"

"I understand we are going broke, but those people in India can't help us with that. What do they know about doing business in America?"

"Yeah, I have ideas on how to save the company lots of money, but the last time someone spoke up around here they got fired. I'm keeping my ideas to myself."

"I have a great idea for a product that would revolutionize our business. But the product development hassle is so bad in this company that it's just not worth it. I am holding onto the idea until we go out of business. Maybe my next employer can help me get the idea to market."

"This company hates old people. I never thought that fifty was old, but now I see it is, at least around here. I give up. Let those inexperienced thirtysomethings take over. I will be here at eight and go home at four thirty and retire at the very first opportunity. Screw them."

These are all statements of resignation. These people are resigned to the status quo. They are beaten down by how they perceive the world. They believe they are powerless. They have given up deep down to their bone marrow. These people are toxic in the workplace.

Why do I bring up resignation when writing about listening? Because these people need enablers to help them become the victims they want to be. Your job is to not be that person. Either point them in a more positive direction or tell them firmly that you do not share their feelings and do not want to continue these conversations. Victims want you to join them in Victim Hell. Avoid the slippery slope.

I have a few more thoughts about resignation.

The victim feels that there is nothing he or she can do (or that the price is too high) to change the situation. Victims need to feel as though someone is persecuting them, such as the boss, management in general or the company as a whole. They also need someone to enable them, a coconspirator.

Victims love to be right. They love to blame others. They

don't want to solve problems; they just want to point them out. In fact, they want the problems to continue so that they can keep blaming others for them.

Victims carry the communicable disease of resignation. They are not complainers or contrarians. I actually love complainers and contrarians. They don't often become very successful, but they do help teams and companies become successful by creating enough tension so that problems are addressed and new avenues are explored. Victims are people who see life as they want to see it and find no hope for improving their lot. They are dashers of hope, and killers of creativity. They can have enormous impact in the workplace, and it's all negative. They spend their days recruiting new victims and gathering evidence to prove themselves right.

You may have picked up on the fact that I don't like victims.

SUSPECT YOURSELF

Let's get personal for a moment. Does any of this sound uncomfortably familiar to you? Are you a victim? If you suspect that you are headed in that direction, it's time to stop, drop and roll. You need to put this fire out now, or it will consume you. Most of the people who share their career concerns with me, who tell me that they are not progressing as fast as they think they should be, are quite far into victimhood. So what do you do if you've become a victim?

First, you need to develop your own radar to help you spot resignation in yourself or others. Are you hearing innocent complaining, or are those words and thoughts really about being powerless to change a bad situation? You can ask a coach or mentor to watch for signs of resignation in you and to point them out to you when they surface. Not to scare you, but at some point almost all of us become resigned about something important. This is not just an exercise for some other person; *suspect yourself.*

YOU CAN RECOVER FROM BEING A VICTIM

If you do find that you are resigned over something, you can recover. Start with a mind-set that says you will not allow yourself to sit on the sidelines and boo the other players. You will not engage in conversations—started by you or by others—that reinforce the feeling of being resigned or of being a victim. You need to be thinking about possibilities, not hopelessness. Remember the Robert Kennedy quote (who actually was quoting from George Bernard Shaw): "Some look at things as they are and ask why. I dream of things that never were and ask why not?" That's the difference between resignation and exploring possibilities.

I know it's sometimes tempting to join in the wallowing. It makes us feel like one of the gang. It gives us a common foe. There is a never-ending supply of things to complain about, and more and more evidence to gather to support those complaints. Resignation becomes a way of life.

I am here to tell you that successful people are not resigned. They are not victims. They see things that are broken and fix them, even when it's really hard to do. They find new ways or try old solutions combined with new technology. Have you ever heard someone say, "That won't work; we tried that already"? That's a sign of resignation. Successful people keep trying until the problem is solved.

Think about it this way. Who do you think is more valuable to the company, a resigned person sitting on the sidelines and doing nothing to improve the situation, or someone who has the guts to roll up his or her sleeves, get in the game, and try things until the problem is solved? If you want a great career, you have to become valuable to the company and to your boss. Resigned people are anti-valuable.

Frank Patalano, my old boss, called resignation "a kind of suspended animation." He was right. And his ability to spot resignation in himself and in others made him highly effective at work—not perfect, but effective. It was part of the reason I loved the guy.

When I say I loved Frank, I mean it. Frank passed away recently. I had a chance to run this chapter by him before he passed. He didn't mind that I shared his story with you. Frank was proud of me for my writing. He was a great friend, a heck of a leader, and a guy who improved his leadership because of some intense coaching. I am thankful to have learned from his mistakes and his recoveries, and I dedicate this part of the book to him.

Here's one last thought on listening: Listening is learning, and learning is the key to getting better at what you do. If you are looking for big-time success, your education should not end when you graduate from high school or college. Your education should end when you do. Lifelong learning is not an option for the successful. It's a way of life. Both Harry Truman and basketball coach John Wooden said something along the lines of, "It's what you learn after you know it all that really counts."

LIFELONG LEARNING IS A WAY OF LIFE FOR WINNERS

Lifelong learning needs to be an action, not just a goal. I made it a priority to get my various companies to sponsor my lifelong education. They sent me to Harvard, to the Kellogg School of Management at Northwestern, to Switzerland for innovation training, to DiBianca-Berkman Group training for various leadership skills, to Malandro training for high performance, to the Disney College Program for customer relations training, to Quality College to learn about the extremely important Quality Process, and to myriad technical courses over a span of forty years. They did so because I asked them to. If you don't ask, you don't get. Ask your company to invest in your lifelong education. If your company says no, get that education anyway—and think about finding a new place to work.

Well, I managed to work a fairly long rant on resignation and another rant on lifelong education into a chapter on listening. That shows you I have some work to do on *focus*, a subject I will address later in the book.

> *"Most of the important things in the world have been accomplished by people who have kept on trying when there seemed to be no hope at all."*
> —Dale Carnegie

CHAPTER FOUR

IT'S A CONFIDENCE GAME.

"It is not the mountain that we conquer, but ourselves."
—Sir Edmund Hillary

I can smell confident people. When you walk in my office your confidence level is the first thing I notice. The business world loves confident people. I love them. Confident people run the world.

Most of the confident people I meet are faking it. They are just as scared of the world as the next person, but they have learned to push that fear into the background so they can reach over their heads and pull themselves up.

CONFIDENCE SELLS

What is the big deal about confidence? Confident people are willing to explore, to lead, to speak up, to try new things, to innovate, to fail, and to get up off the ground and try again. Confident people can make a business vision sound like the promised land. People can't wait to line up behind them to go along on the trip.

Saying "I think we can" does not enlist followers as well as saying "I know we can." Confidence gives us the courage to move forward. Confidence is a wonderful thing.

So how do you gain confidence, especially if you are brand new on the job? Well, you start off with some, and you end up with lots.

On day one, you just need to recognize that you have made it this far in life so you must be doing something right. You are confident that you can learn, that you can follow instructions, that you are smart and will become smarter.

Every day you spend on the job, your confidence should grow. Learn to quietly celebrate every little victory, because every little victory will add to your confidence. Try to do new things. Push your envelope. Expand your knowledge and your skills. Become an expert at something—anything. If you are the only one in the office who knows how to fix the stupid copy machine, well, that's something. Your confidence grows when people start coming to you for help. Confident people can do things that other people can't do or aren't willing to try.

FAILURE IS AN IMPORTANT PART OF THE JOURNEY TO SUCCESS

How are you at failing? Here is the biggest secret in business: confident people are pretty good at failing. God knows I've had my share of failures along the way. My good friend Lynn Lyen once said to me, "The thing I like most about you is that you never let your numerous failures stand in the way of your eventual success." I think that was a compliment. I took it as such.

COURAGE IS NEEDED AND IS IN SHORT SUPPLY

This might be a good spot for another side trip. I want to introduce you to the concept of the top 1 percent. I promise I will weave this concept back into the topic at hand.

When you get near the top in Corporate America you finally figure out that the top person in the company does not make just 5 percent more than the number-two person. He or she makes twice as much or more than the number-two person. I wonder what Michael Jordan made compared to Scottie Pippen when they were number-one and number-two on the Chicago Bulls? I will bet their earnings were not even close. Being the best at almost anything pays huge.

I always strive to be in the top 1 percent of everything I do. Why? Because the top 1 percent gets most of the pie. And if you ever make it to the number-one spot, the sky is the limit. Being at the top is a very, very good thing. You might want to weave this into your own definition of success, getting inside that little circle called the top 1 percent. There is gold in that circle.

I bring this up here because you don't get inside that little circle without a heck of a lot of courage. To say out loud that you have set a goal of becoming number-one at anything is a very courageous thing to do. When you make such a declaration, your friends, enemies, relatives, and fellow workers won't necessarily all line up to salute you. In fact, a bunch of them will ridicule you in order to discourage you. There is a brilliant piece of comedy by George Lopez called "Team Leader." Find it and give it a listen. It is a perfect demonstration of what I am trying to describe. George gets named a team leader and his own grandmother immediately starts tearing him down. You don't know whether to laugh or cry at his comedy bit, but you can tell it came out of a real-life experience. We will all have experiences similar to his and we will not be laughing when they happen to us.

People will bring out their weapons of mass discouragement if you declare your intentions of becoming the best. It's kind of like the old story of the crabs boiling in a pot. If one crab tries to crawl out of the boiling pot, the other crabs will pull him back. Crabs and people are a lot alike in that regard.

Part of having confidence is getting over the fear of failure and the fear of ridicule. Consider this quotes from Allen H. Neuharth: "I quit being afraid when my first venture failed and the sky didn't fall down." And this one from Paul Tillich: "Life shrinks or expands in proportion to one's courage."

Of all the things I will cover in this book, courage, I think, is the most rare element in the workplace. The top dogs have it. Some have way too much. But most of us lack it. And only *you* can make *you* courageous.

I suspect you know whether you have courage or whether you don't. Ask yourself a few questions:

1. Am I willing to share my innermost dreams for business success with the people around me? Can I say them out loud?

2. Do I feel I can take a risk at work and survive a failure?

3. How would I react if people I care about laugh at my dreams or make fun of me for my failures?

4. How good am I at getting up from defeat and getting right back into the battle?

Whether you do or don't have confidence today, you need to get to a point where you can express your ideas for success and handle risk, ridicule, and defeat—handle them and not let any of them discourage you.

I promise you that people I really care about have laughed in my face and told me that I could not possibly do the thing I dreamed of doing. I didn't stop loving them. I just went about my business and succeeded anyway.

Confidence comes from trying and doing, from saying and then delivering, from failing once but winning in the end. Confidence builds slowly and can be lost in an instant. When it is gone, bad things ensue. Successful people get back on the horse after they are thrown off and ride on toward the next task. Sometimes they ride on with a bit less confidence and a sore posterior. But they ride nonetheless. Confidence will return. It has in the past, and it will again.

Let me make one more aside before we head into another area. I want to take a few minutes to discuss confidence that is not real and confidence that has become way too real.

I think that people who make a big public display of their confidence are usually faking real confidence and are usually a major pain in the ass at work. They try to look confident by being bullies, by acting like they are some kind of dictator, by diminishing you, and by having all the answers. They talk big and then never stick their necks out. I guarantee you that they will never stick their necks out *for you*. These fakes are everywhere at work. They are major sources of bitterness, discontent, and unnecessary turbulence in the workplace. Watch out for them, and for God's sake, don't become one of them. It's fine to show your vulnerability, but they don't have the guts to do it.

ARROGANCE IS EVIL

And at the other end of the spectrum are the arrogant. They take up too much space and are not worth the air they breathe. These little tin soldiers need to be run out of town at the end of a pointy stick. Arrogant people don't listen to anyone but themselves. They are completely unaware or uncaring about *their impact on others*. They do such things as making everyone wait an hour while they do whatever they want to do, interrupting the speaker and taking over the rest of the meeting, or picking at you in public until everyone in the room just wants to hide under the table. They grab all the perks, goodies, and glory for themselves.

You've met these people, or you will soon. Early in your career, there's not much you can do to change them. Nevertheless, heed these couple of pleas from me: Don't let them scare you from contributing at work. And never become one of these people yourself. My theory is that they are either completely lacking in self-confidence or just plain evil. Either way, outlive them and enjoy the last laugh.

You need confidence to succeed at work—even though we all have flaws. It's a very flawed world. But winners move ahead with confidence despite their imperfections and occasional mistakes and failures. That is what makes us winners.

"Courage is being scared to death and saddling up anyway."
—John Wayne

CHAPTER FIVE

INSTALL A PERISCOPE IN YOUR CUBICLE.

*"The World is a book, and those who
do not travel read only a page."*
—St. Augustine

LEARN MORE THAN JUST YOUR OWN JOB

The biggest winners in Corporate America understand how the whole mechanism works. By that I mean they understand

- How the economy works

- How the industry works

- How the company works and makes its money

- How the department works and makes its money

- How the various parts of the organization work and work together to do the whole job.

These winners know who the players are in the company and throughout the whole industry. They work to understand it all so that someday they can run it all.

That all sounds so easy and so logical. The problem is most people don't bother to learn these things. They focus hard on the inbox or their electronic queue, do their work, and are really too busy to be bothered by any other stuff.

When I was in charge of communications of a company I sought to understand how people receive information at work. I soon discovered that you can produce a ton of information for people to see, listen to, or read, but that does not ensure they will actually receive that information. Their number-one source of information is their direct boss.

It turns out that the direct boss filters much of the incoming information and passes on only those tidbits that he or she thinks people need to know—and that turns out to be information that is highly focused on the job at hand. As a result, people know lots about the job at hand, some about what is going on elsewhere in the division, a rare piece of information from some other part of the company, and only the headlines about what is happening in the overall company or industry.

Let me get even more specific. On my first day as CEO of a sizable profit center within a much larger company, I visited one of my offices in another state. This was a fairly small office and located on one floor of a building. I came in the front door and asked the first person I met where I could find the branch manager. He had no idea. I mentioned the person by name, but he still had no idea where to find him. Then I wandered around the office until I found someone who knew where to find the person I was seeking. It took me five long minutes.

The problem was that I had asked someone in another department to point me toward the branch manager. Even though there were fewer than one hundred people in this outpost, they communicated only with the people in their own departments and never bothered to meet other people in the office. I ran into this problem at other companies too. It was disgusting, but real.

While I am venting, let me tell you about the time I went to our downtown flagship office and asked someone where I could find the people there who worked for me. Again, this person had no idea. He said I might try the next floor up, that he heard our company had space there. I asked him how long he had been with the company. "Twenty years," he said proudly. Twenty years, and he had never been to that floor way up there, twelve feet above his head.

It probably won't surprise you to learn that our operation was losing money in part because the different departments did not work well together. They did duplicate training, had duplicate equipment and duplicate jobs, and no synergy whatsoever.

These types of problems start by people choosing to never look outside of their cubicle. It is safe and warm in there. If they don't look around they will probably be left alone and won't have to do any extra work. Hopefully, people won't notice them, and that will keep them safe when it comes time to downsize.

Lay low, keep a low profile, do my job, and do nothing more. Keep an eye on that clock. Hot dog, it's five o'clock, time to quietly leave and go home. I think I will leave my computer on in case the boss comes by my cubicle. Maybe she will think I am still here.

Don't think I am exaggerating. If you are just beginning your career, you'll see this kind of behavior yourself very soon.

I once transferred to an office where the workers were known throughout the company for not playing well with others and for operating as though they were all on the time clock. On my first day there, I ran up the back stairs to get up to the CEO's office, at 4:30 p.m. The doors opened above me, and I was very nearly trampled. By 4:35 p.m. the stairwell was vacant, the floors of the office were vacant, the parking lot was vacant, and my hopes for the future of this office were vacant.

The CEO had no idea. He was a really busy guy and never really looked up from his office until he was ready to go home, fairly late at night. At 4:30 pm the next afternoon I physically dragged him to that stairwell. It was like standing at the entrance of a bat cave just as the sun goes down. It was quite an eye opener for my boss and quite a nasty experience for me.

The point is we all need to have our periscopes up so we can see outside of our immediate environment and understand what is going on in the business. Here is a game plan to help you get ahead of your competition in this all-important area:

1. Take a course in economics so you will know how the economy works.

If you took economics in college and actually understood it, skip to the next point. If you didn't take it or didn't really understand the concepts taught, go back to school and take it seriously. Economics are the foundation of understanding how business works in this world. If you don't have a good grasp of the basics of economics, you will be passed by those who do. Successful businesspeople understand economics.

2. Understand your industry.

I spent my first twenty-seven years at work with one of America's great companies. I won't mention its name (Allstate) because that just wouldn't be fair. As good as this company was at the time, its executives had one significant fault. They wanted their people to look to the company for everything. They didn't want us to be involved in the industry beyond the tasks that were directly in front of us. In fact, for my first several years at Allstate, I had no idea how the rest of the industry worked, or what opportunities were out there that I was missing.

A wonderful boss of mine, Don Weiland, took me to my first industry function. What an awakening for me! I met people from companies I never knew existed who did exactly the same job I was doing. I met people in related jobs who seemed to be making a lot more money than I was making. It turned out there was a whole world of opportunity out there to explore. Attending that event changed my life.

Allstate may have been wise in trying to keep us

sequestered. My exposure to the outside world led me to finally leave Allstate, just twenty-seven years after joining the company.

Know your industry. Be involved in it in some way. Join an industry group. Attend seminars. Network. Read the trade press. Stay connected every single day of your career. If you know how the industry works, you'll understand the decisions that your company makes in a much more holistic way. You'll understand trends that threaten your job or that create opportunities for you. And you will know people who can help you when you need help.

3. Know how your company makes its money.

Most people have no idea how their company really makes money. If you want to read an interesting book on the subject, look for Jack Stack's *The Great Game of Business*. Jack saved a company from going out of business by teaching every person in the company, including the janitor, how the company makes its money. His open-book style of management enabled him and the company to survive and ultimately to succeed. Your understanding of the financial workings of your company will do the same for you.

Start by reading what others say about your company from a financial point of view. Check out Internet sources of information such as Yahoo!

Finance or the Motley Fool. See what the analysts have to say. Read and seek to understand the financial highlights.

I am an avid reader of annual reports, especially the ones of the company that employs me and the ones of its leading competitors. I don't just thumb through them; I read them carefully and then find a CFO type to help me understand the parts I don't understand.

Your company doesn't make money by just selling widgets or whatever. It makes money by investing, by selling assets and leasing them back, by cutting expenses, by taking advantage of various tax breaks, by creating profits and losses at the right time of year. There is a lot to learn in this area—a lifetime of learning.

Here is one guarantee: No one becomes the CEO of a significant company without knowing how that company makes its money. No one, that is, except for the daughter or son of the founder, who still controls all of the stock. Unless you are that daughter or son, learn how your firm makes its money. Successful people understand the financials.

4. Know how your company's other departments operate.

You may be in sales, but what do the people in manufacturing do? How about the legal department? What do the lawyers really do? What about the finance guys, the investment team, the folks in marketing, communications, advertising, mergers and acquisitions, and on and on. It may take you years to really know what each department does and how they all fit together, but it will be time well spent. People who end up running businesses know how the parts of the whole mechanism fit together. They know who the superstars are within their own department and elsewhere. They have enough knowledge to help the company become more effective and cost-efficient by having departments work better together.

There is more to your business than what you can see through the little window that looks out on your department and your department only.

It's time for another aside.

I have spent my entire career sizing up my competition. I started by thinking of my competitors at work as a pie, or rather a pie chart.

How was I going to get past this pie of people to get the jobs and success I so desired? Part of the answer came from item number four, from learning how all of the company's departments operated. The people who fail to look up and out of their own cubicle, who never give one thought outside their own department, that piece of the pie is *huge*. These folks don't even know who the CEO is, or what the person on the next floor does for a living. They have no idea how helpful the information they have at hand would be to someone else in another part of the company. They are clueless and they are legion. You will surge by them if you take the initiative to understand the whole mechanism. And when the day comes that they are competing with you for the kind of jobs that manage multiple functions, these shortsighted folks will see you fly right by. Of course, they won't even know your name or what you use to do for a living. They might not even see you. Remember, they never look much past their own nose.

If you'd like some proof that a large number of your competitors are clueless, here it is. In my last days in Corporate America, when I was 61 years old and trying to wrap up one last assignment before retiring, my company named a new CEO. The guy was young, good-looking, exceedingly bright and had a wonderful education and résumé. The day after the announcement of his promotion three people stopped me in the halls to congratulate *me* on becoming CEO. Clueless, each of them.

I thought for a moment about having some fun with the situation. I strongly considered telling them to get back to work and to never make eye contact with me again. I'll bet that word would have gotten around the office pretty quickly! Instead, I smiled, thanked them and secretly wished that they had been correct.

5. Know how your company's other profit centers operate.

Allstate ran multiple businesses. I worked for only one. And in those days the company was owned by Sears. Sears was in hundreds of businesses. Another of my companies, Zurich Financial Services, once ran 365 profit centers, everything from banks to insurance companies all around the world. I made it my business to know something and someone at almost all those businesses.

The easiest place to look for solutions to any problem you face at work is within your own company. If you need to enter a new business, find a way to cut costs or hire new talent, it is easiest if you know where to find the appropriate expertise or resources within your own company. Knowing all of your company's resources might even become important if something awkward happens, like you find you are going to lose your job in the upcoming reorganization.

Remember the pie chart? Another big slice of competitors never bothers to make any connections or learn anything at all about the other important businesses that are part of your overall company. Exploit that lack of knowledge. Know your company.

Too many people think it is their job to just do the work that is placed in front of them. They have no interest in doing anything else. As soon as you put up your periscope and start learning how the world outside of your cubicle works, you begin to distance yourself from a great big pie-chart piece of the competition. Go "up periscope" and move ahead five spaces. Collect the $200 for passing "Go," and then prepare to collect much more in the future. There is gold in understanding how the economy, industry, and the various parts of your business really work. Mine the gold.

"The whole purpose of education is to turn mirrors into windows."
—Sydney J. Harris

CHAPTER SIX

WE ARE ON A MISSION.

"If you are ashamed to stand by your colors,
you had better seek another flag."
—Author unknown

KNOW YOUR PURPOSE

Here is another simple thing we all can do to put our heads and shoulders ahead of the competition at work: Understand and be able to articulate and support the mission statement and vision of your company.

This is easy to do, and yet almost no one does it. It also gives you the kind of purpose you need to make your job enjoyable. Lastly, this is a skill you will absolutely need to possess when you begin to achieve success and start to take over the world.

I spent many long hours in rooms filled with very bright and fabulously paid people, working with them to craft company mission and vision statements. You know the kind of statements I am talking about, the ones designed to tell employees and the outside world exactly what the company is in business to do. Here is what I learned from this experience: Writing an effective mission or vision statement is not easy. Most are too long and complex for anyone to understand and support. There are a few exceptions. What follows are statements that are clear and concise and help people to understand the mission. They may not be complete or current, but they help me illustrate the qualities of an effective mission statement.

3M: "To solve unsolved problems innovatively."

Mary Kay Cosmetics: "To give unlimited opportunities to women."

Merck: "To preserve and protect human life."

Walmart: "To give ordinary folk the chance to buy the same thing as rich people."

Walt Disney: "To make people happy."

Each of these one-liners tells a story. Add to these statements the plans and tactics of the company, and their employees can understand what they are hired to do and how they are going to do it.

I might mention that not all mission statements are quite as informative as the preceding examples. Here is a beauty I recently discovered: "It is our mission to dramatically initiate performance based opportunities as well as to proactively leverage existing quality leadership skills to meet our customer's needs." Say what?

In addition to crafting several mission statements in my career, I also got to see how the different companies introduced and reinforced those messages. To say that not every company got it right would be a massive understatement.

Try this with your circle of friends, the ones who have jobs and who you think are the most professional. Ask them to tell you their companies' mission statements. It will be even more informative and fun if you can ask this question to two people who work for the same company.

I've sat in board meetings where the directors could not even come close to reciting or paraphrasing their company's mission. I've attended senior staff meetings in which the executives could not remember the mission. I've attended hundreds of meetings where the attendees had no idea of the company's mission. It is all very frustrating to me, and to bosses like me.

BE ON A MISSION

The company pays your salary. Part of the quid pro quo for that payment is that you understand what the company intends to accomplish and what your job is in support of those goals. If you are showing up each day only to "do work," you are not on a mission, and you will never have the success you desire.

Here is the good news: This is another big-pieces-of-the-pie item that can put you way ahead of your competitors at work. I am telling you that very few people understand the mission of their company, much less the plans and tactics put in place to accomplish that mission. If you work with your boss until you understand that mission and those plans—understand them well enough to easily articulate them to others, and understand exactly what job you need to do to help bring the mission alive—you will be on your way to becoming a superstar. Your boss will love you. Your boss's boss will love you. And you will love your job.

One of the first things bosses look for when determining who they should train and eventually promote into supervisory and management positions is someone who understands what the company is working to accomplish, someone who supports the vision and can communicate that vision to others. Successful people are the carriers of that flame. They understand, can articulate, and support the vision of the company. That is one of the first definitions of a leader, someone who can carry the vision and can enroll others in carrying that vision. If you are in that small group early on, you will be well on your way to success in the workplace.

> *"I know the price of success: dedication, hard work, and an unremitting devotion to the things you want to see happen"*
> —Frank Lloyd Wright

PART TWO

EXPAND YOUR OPPORTUNITIES FOR FUTURE SUCCESS

Did you ever hear the story about the man who prayed to God every day that he would win the lottery?

Despite his prayers, the poor guy just never won. After years of frustration, he went out to the middle of the woods and shouted at God, "I pray and pray, and you just leave me here poor as ever. Why, God, don't you ever answer my prayers?"

God answered, "I'm willing to help, but *you* have to buy a ticket."

That is what this section of the book is all about. It's about you buying a ticket, a ticket to a successful career. And the good news is that many of your competitors at work will never get into the ticket line.

CHAPTER SEVEN

GOALS ARE GOOD. NO GOALS EQUALS NO SUCCESS.

"Shoot for the moon. Even if you miss, you'll land among the stars."
—Les Brown

LEARN TO SET GOALS EFFECTIVELY

Someone had to teach me to set goals. Until I reached high school, no one had even mentioned goals to me. I really didn't see the need for them and certainly did not understand their power. The only goals I knew about were for weight watchers. And since I weighted only 118 pounds as a freshman in high school, goals were not for me.

When I reflected on goals later in life, I realized that I did have a goal early on. It was a really small and unimportant goal, but it was a goal, and it was important to me. I wanted to be the fastest runner in the school. Let me rephrase that: I wanted to *remain* the fastest runner in the school.

I had earned the title of the fastest kid in kindergarten when I beat the second-fastest kid, my girlfriend, Mary Zema, in my very first race. Not that I was competitive, or obnoxious, but I made every new kid who transferred into our school race me on his or her first day, just to get the fastest-kid pecking order all squared away. I'm sure that several of those kids are still seeing a psychiatrist to deal with the scars left by that little initiation ritual.

When I got to high school, the goal became a bit more difficult to achieve. I eventually went out for the track team and met the great big scary coach, Bill O'Rourke. Coach O'Rourke watched me run and jump in practice. He then asked me to run over some hurdles, something I had never done in my life. After I managed to make it past the hurdles without killing myself, he asked me to join him in his office.

The coach asked me if I had any goals. I told him about my goal to be the fastest kid in our school. He told me, this 118-pound kid, that I should set my goals a wee bit higher. Based on what he just witnessed, he felt I should set a goal of becoming an Olympic champion. That advice changed my life.

I won't bore you by telling you how close I came to achieving that goal. Besides, I tend to exaggerate my track accomplishments every time I tell the story. In fact, after listening to me mention some of my track accomplishments in a speech a few years ago, Coach O'Rourke told me that I had gotten a lot faster over the years. It suffices to say that I don't have any Olympic gold medals, but I shot for the moon and did become a star—fairly low magnitude, but a star nonetheless. I am forever thankful that Coach O'Rourke got me thinking like a champion.

Do you have a Coach O'Rourke in your life, someone who

pushes you out of your comfort zone and causes you to think *big*? If not, let me be your coach. I would love to help you think about some goals that are big enough to require a lifetime of work, really big goals that will lead to really big success.

Let me warm you up with some thoughts by some exceedingly bright people. The first is from Zig Ziglar who said, "I don't care how much power, brilliance or energy you have. If you don't harness it and focus it on a specific target, and hold it there, you're never going to accomplish as much as your ability warrants." The second is from Charles C. Noble. He said, "You must have long-term goals to keep you from being frustrated by short-term failures."

I can tell you from my years of being a boss, coach, and mentor at work that most of your competition at work will not be very good at setting long-term goals. If you can do that, you can pull away from the competition.

Most of the goals I heard were incremental, such as, "I hope to one day have your job." That one usually came from someone who reported directly to me. Rising just one more level over the course of an entire career is not much of a goal.

As for those less senior in the company who spoke to me about their goals, their aspirations also were often unspectacular. Even the rare few who told me that they one day wanted to own the company or be the chairman or chairwoman would quickly add something like, "But becoming a department manager would be just fine."

I rarely heard anyone mention anything grand and inspiring. My bet is that many people had such goals, but they were not willing to share them with me.

SET SOME BIG GOALS . . . GOALS THAT MIGHT TAKE A LIFETIME OF WORK TO ACHIEVE

If you want to remain motivated for your entire career, set a grand goal. Share that goal with others. Begin to do the work that will move you toward that goal. And *never ever give up* on it. You will be amazed at what you can accomplish over the course of a lifetime of work.

Here are a few more suggestions: Write down the biggest goal for yourself that you can dream up. Don't filter that goal with what you think is reasonable, realistic or acceptable to others. What would absolutely thrill you when you actually achieve it?

I'll tell you one of my goals. I intend to win an Oscar for a screenplay or song that I write. That's a sizable goal for a guy over sixty years of age who has never done anything in the movie industry and has no prospects of doing so. Still, I am dead serious about reaching that goal, and I will do the work to make it happen.

Yours can't be more outrageous than mine. So blurt it out. What is it that you want more than anything in the world? If you can't write it down and eventually tell it to others, it ain't going to happen.

HOW TO SET GOALS

Here is a step-by-step game plan for putting your grand goals in place and in play.

Step one: Write down your grand goal or goals. By the way, it doesn't have to be completely specific; directional is just as good. For example, you might say that you will become the CEO of one of America's biggest companies, as opposed to saying, "I will become the CEO of Google."

Step two: Share your goals with others. Learn to steel yourself against those who will seek to dash your dreams. Learn to spot those who will support your efforts to make your dreams come true. Listen for the feedback to help you identify the hurdles you might encounter along the way to success.

I actually think that people can do anything they set their mind to doing. I had a boss who became a very senior executive at a very large company despite a significant stuttering problem. I've had plenty of ugly bosses, and I'm no beauty. I had a terrific boss—a very successful guy—who was about five foot two and another who played with *Star Wars* toys in his office (I saw recently that he is making way over two million dollars a year). All kinds of people enjoy tremendous success. And you fit in the category of "all kinds of people." Set big goals and don't blink when you tell others about your dreams. You are as likely to hit those goals as anyone else—*if* you actually have a dream.

And remember that when you have done all the work and have finally reached your goals, don't spit on the dreams of others. Remember how special it was when someone encouraged you. Pay it down the line. Listen to others' goals with an ear toward helping them make their dreams come true. *Encourage* beats *discourage* every time.

Step three: Get a coach to help you as you craft plans to meet your goals. I'm going to talk more about this step in the next chapter.

Step four: Craft a plan to start moving toward your goals. The goals might be as simple as these:

1. Become the CEO of a manufacturing company by the time I am forty.

2. Use the CEO platform to put into play my views on the importance of diversity in the workplace.

3. Use any excess money I earn to fund scholarships for Mexican-American students who want to go to college and cannot afford to do so.

Step five: Turn the goals into action steps that will bring the plan alive. Here's an example of action steps for the goals stated in step four:

1. Go to work for a manufacturing company that has an excellent reputation for developing the industry's most respected leaders.

2. Go back to college and earn an MBA.

3. Find a mentor to help me move to the next step in my development.

Note that the game plan does not have to take you all the way to the final goal. It only needs to put you well on that path.

Step six: Work the plan. Establish some measures for your progress. A goal or game plan without due dates and deadlines is only a dream. Also, meet with your coach or mentor regularly to discuss your progress and to establish the next steps. Make adjustments as necessary. Enjoy your progress.

You are in competition with all those other good folks in your office and many others. You need to find ways to eventually move ahead of *all* of them. One of those ways is to have grand goals and a plan to reach those goals. Your competitors will think you are smoking dope. Their lack of faith in your ability to reach your grand goals is no reason to hate them. It is, however, a really good reason to enjoy the moment when you breeze past them. Then you will never need to look back, only forward to the next hurdle and your next success.

"The world is moving so fast these days that the man who says it can't be done is generally interrupted by someone doing it."
—Elbert Hubbard

CHAPTER EIGHT

COACHES ARE AS VALUABLE AS GOLD TO YOU.

"A good coach will make his players see what they can be rather than what they are."
—Ara Parseghian

I have been blessed with terrific coaches in my life. First and always, I have my parents. Next I had a few special teachers along the way. In sports, I had several coaches who made a huge difference in my life. The same was true at work.

I want to make a case for your having a coach, to give you some ideas on how to find a coach who will be willing to work with you, and to suggest how you might get the most out of that relationship.

Remember Coach O'Rourke, who I mentioned in an earlier chapter? He remained my coach until the day he died, just a couple of years ago.

YOUR COACH WILL OFFER A NEW PERSPECTIVE

Coach O'Rourke helped me see things about myself that I couldn't see on my own. I wanted to be a high jumper and sprinter. He saw that I wasn't a good high jumper, but I was a fairly good sprinter. He suggested I try something that involved both sprinting and jumping—the hurdles. It turns out that I was an excellent hurdler. I would never have made the change on my own.

Coach O'Rourke helped me to think beyond my own frame of reference. He had coached Olympians. He saw that I shared some of the talents enjoyed by those athletes. He convinced me to stop thinking about being the best in the school and to start thinking about being the best in the world. He arranged for me to meet the world's best at my event so that I could see he was actually just a fellow human being. Coach helped me to visualize my becoming a champion.

YOUR COACH WILL PUSH YOU TO EXPAND YOUR LIMITS

Coach O'Rourke made me learn the basics. Oh, I hated doing the basics of my event day after day after day. I hated doing fifteen starts a day over the first hurdle, hated going back each time to see where my footsteps were on the track, hated making those little tiny adjustments. The funny thing is those tiny little adjustments and careful attention to the basics were often what separated me from my competitors. I've been in the finals of important hurdle races in which first place and last place were separated by only two-tenths of a second. The little things do count. Sometimes they are the difference between winning and losing.

Coach encouraged me to work incredibly hard—unreasonably hard, I thought. We worked so hard that I would often throw up during the workouts. I never would have pushed myself so hard. It takes a coach to get a person to move well beyond his or her comfort zone.

One of the coaches I most admire is Steve Simmons. He is also a great friend. Steve has served as the manager of the U.S. Olympic track and field team. He was my coach in college. There are three things that I will never forget about Steve.

First, he never said a word when I showed up at practice extremely hungover on my twenty-first birthday. He did, however, work me until my body was purged of all alcohol, food, and a few vital organs. There was a lesson there: a coach will make you work hard even when you have no intention of doing so.

The second memory involves the time I was injured in a workout and had to have several stitches in my heel. The next day we had a fairly unimportant meet. I offered to be a timer or to keep score. Coach had a better idea. He wanted me to run all of my events. Again, that's not something I would have done on my own. But guess what? I ran one of my fastest times of the year, and it really added to my confidence. And having the stitches put back into my heel after they were torn out during the meet was not as painful as I thought it would be.

The third memory is from my senior year, when I had a successful showing at the NCAA Division Two Regional Championships. I medaled in the 100, the hurdles, and the 4 x 100 relay.

It was a good day's work, and I was a happy camper. I was happy until Coach Simmons told me to put my shoes back on and get ready to run a 440 yard leg in the 4 x 440 relay. I cannot tell you how much I hated to run the quarter mile. It made me sick every time I ran it—sick enough to vomit. I told Coach no. He reached down and picked up my spikes. I guessed what he was about to do with those spikes, which was to beat me with them until I was fully tenderized, and rethought my decision. Today, I have one extra NCAA regional medal in my house because I had a coach who wouldn't let me take the easy way out.

I picked the three preceding anecdotes to illustrate how a great coach can push you past your own barriers. It may sound as though Coach Simmons was a brute, but high-level sports is a very tough business. A coach can't be just nice and supportive; often he or she has to be firm and demanding. Coach Simmons was always up for being firm and demanding.

That said, I have never had a coach do more for me than Coach Simmons did. We remain very good friends some forty years later. He still coaches me today—about life. He always makes me feel respected and appreciated for my hard work and accomplishments. He still knows how to push me to do better. He shares his friends, his network of associates, and his opportunities with me. I am extremely thankful for his being in my life. And yes, he still scares me just a little.

Back to the lessons learned from Coach O'Rourke.

He taught me to set goals and to measure my progress. To this day, I still write down my goals and keep a journal of my progress. He also taught me to "panic early." If I wasn't making progress early on, he said, then make changes right away to turn the situation around. This advice turned out to be more helpful in business than it was in athletics. I learned to panic early when sales were down at work. Too many of my competitors waited to see what the next quarter would bring. By then it usually was too late.

YOUR COACH WILL MEASURE YOUR PROGRESS

Coach O'Rourke gave me completely honest feedback. He told me the truth. He told me when I did something great. He told me when I was not making progress. He let me know when I disappointed him and when I made him proud. He told me how I was doing in comparison with the competition. He never held back the truth. Great coaches tell you the truth, even when the truth hurts.

He taught me to visualize winning. He actually had me spend a good part of one day a week lying in the stands with my eyes closed, creating little videos in my head. Each video featured me winning an important race. I knew what it looked and felt like to win before I ever put a foot on the track. If you can see it, you can do it.

Coach O'Rourke taught me to be organized and prepared. That little lesson has paid off well throughout my life. By the way, I did not want to be organized and prepared. He just wouldn't work with me if I did not bend to his will on this important subject. I learned to value a coach's help above my own selfish or lazy desires.

He taught me to be a gracious winner. I was not allowed to make my competitors feel any worse about losing to me. They already felt bad. Thanks to Coach's help, I have managed to stay friends with some of my fiercest competitors to this day.

By the way, Coach O'Rourke never taught me to be a good loser. First off, I didn't lose very often. When I did, I never used an excuse. If I lost, he taught me, I lost. We had to get back to work and figure out how to win next time around. I was never a loser—even when I lost.

A GREAT COACH WILL ENCOURAGE YOU TO THINK ABOUT THE GOOD YOU CAN DO WITH YOUR SUCCESS

Coach O'Rourke encouraged me and made me feel special. He was never about himself; he was always about his athletes. He patted us on the back, gave out awards, made us feel like winners. He continued to do so throughout his life.

He introduced the idea of doing something special with my success. When I called him to tell him I had just made CEO, he congratulated me warmly and reminded me of how hard I had worked to reach this grand goal. And then I will be darned if he didn't slip this in: "Don, what are you going to do with this great opportunity? Is this one of the places where you can help your company increase the diversity of its executive staff? Are there some high-potential young people who you can mentor?" That was quite a talent; he could congratulate me and coach me at the same time.

I loved Coach O'Rourke, and I miss him every single day.

So this is what a coach does:

- Helps you see things about yourself that you can't see on your own

- Inspires you to think beyond your own frame of reference

- Ensures that you are a master of the basics

- Makes you work harder than you would on your own

- Helps you to set goals and establish measures

- Provides completely truthful feedback on your performance

- Keeps you so focused on being successful that you can actually feel, see, and taste victory, even before you reach your goal

- Insists that you be organized and prepared

- Helps you become a gracious winner and a no-excuses loser

- Always encourages you and makes you feel special

- Helps you to see new possibilities once you have achieved initial success

I have been blessed with a number of coaches or mentors at work who, like Coach O'Rourke and Coach Simmons, made me better. Each had a special area of expertise and used it to help me make a breakthrough in my career.

GETTING A COACH OR A MENTOR

With many things in life, if you don't ask, you don't get. That's the case with a coach or mentor.

If you wait for the company to assign a mentor as part of its should-have-been-launched-two-decades-ago mentors program, it may be a long wait. Your career is too important for you to rely on an HR or personnel department. *You* are responsible for recruiting a coach.

Who should you recruit? Well, take a look at the list of things I said that Coach O'Rourke did for me. Think about people you trust, admire and respect—people who are likely candidates for the unpaid job as your coach. One word of warning: these should be people you want in your life forever. Choose a coach carefully. If you are lucky enough to find a great coach, be smart enough to hire him or her for life.

Once you have identified a prospect or prospects, have a conversation with them. Ask if they are interested in becoming your coach. When you have signed someone up for the job, establish some rules of engagement, such as how often you will meet and how open you are to feedback.

If your company does have a mentor program, sign up for it. The mentor programs I've seen are excellent.

Once you have a coach in your corner, take that relationship seriously. Give back for his or her involvement. Give your thanks. Brag about your coach to others. Let your coach know how highly you value the relationship. Coaching relationships need to contain something for the coach as well as the coached.

Are you serious about becoming successful at work? If you are, taking the step of hiring a coach shows the world that you are serious. This is yet another way that you can leave competitors in your dust. Many of your competitors will never develop a serious coach/mentor relationship. You will. And you will win.

Did you know that the great golfer Phil Mickelson has a golf coach? Why does he need a coach? For the same reason you do. He wants to be the absolute best that he can be. It has worked out fairly well for him, and it will work out well for you. Get a coach.

"I never cease to be amazed at the power of the coaching process to draw out the skills or talent that was previously hidden within an individual . . . "
—John Russell

CHAPTER NINE

NETWORK LIKE YOUR SUCCESS DEPENDS ON IT.

*"Poverty, I realized, wasn't only a lack of financial resources;
it was isolation from the kind of people that could help
you make more of yourself."*
—Keith Ferrazzi

For years I ran a network called the UFOD—the Unemployed Friends of Don. Sometimes the network was empty. Often it was well populated. People were always coming and going.

UFODs are some of my best friends. We all made our livings in a tough industry—insurance. Companies grew and shrank, came and went, or turned out to be poor fits for UFODs. These folks needed jobs.

I was exceedingly pleased and privileged to run this network. I honestly believe that the following quote from Edgar Watson Howe should be a way of life: "When a friend is in trouble, don't annoy him by asking if there is anything you can do. Think up something appropriate and do it."

I thought up something appropriate. I hired these people if I needed them. I paid them a fair wage. I hired them as consultants at first. If someone turned out to be an outstanding fit and could provide great value, I hired him or her into something permanent. In the meantime, I had an understanding with UFODs that they could continue to look for full-time employment and could leave if they needed. All I wanted was their best work while they were under contract.

Please note that I never hired anyone who I did not actually need. I was hiring these people with the companies' money, not my own. These hires were never a gift, and I always got good value for the arrangement.

UFODs are just a small part of my overall network. I am proud to say that I put together a huge network over my forty years in business. And the network served me well.

THE CASE FOR BEING A NETWORKER

A network is a resource—a very valuable resource. Carefully built and constantly nurtured, it will become a major part of your eventual success. With the help of a robust network, you can do the following:

- Find people to hire

- Check out the reputation of someone you might hire

- Find expertise when you need it in a hurry

- Have someone to talk to when you need to check out a business-related rumor or to get more information than is provided in a press release

- Find out what the competition is doing

- Talk to someone who can help you get a new job

- Get some coaching

- Provide some coaching

- Have someone to talk to when you really need to speak with someone

Winners are highly networked. There is a great book by Keith Ferrazzi called *Never Eat Alone*. Pick up the book and read it and live it. It will tell you all you need to know about networking and how to be an effective networker.

How do you start a network? A great place is your first orientation class or first training class at work. Pick out a few of the brighter bulbs in that string and stay in touch with them forever. If they eventually leave the company, stay in touch. Make sure you find a way to touch base with each person at least once a quarter.

Every time you do something special—attend a class, go to a seminar, call on clients—build your network. Build it forever.

NETWORKING PERSONALITIES

There are three kinds of networkers:

Networking Black Belts network easily. It's second nature to them. They seem to know everyone, and everyone knows them. They are visible in the industry and the community. They are movers and shakers. My advice: earn your networking black belt.

Networking White Belts are shy. They want to network, but they don't have the confidence to do the things necessary to build the network relationships. They don't want to bother people. They would call someone important, but they don't really know what to say. They would love to call and ask for a favor, but they are afraid that person will want something in return. Sometimes they start off well, but then they get busy and let the contacts and relationships wither and die. If this sounds like you, do some studying on networking. Ask your coach to help you in this area. Redouble your efforts. You can do this right. Successful people don't wear white belts.

Networking No Belts are my least favorites. I've told this story before, and I will tell it again. When I left Allstate in Chicago after twenty-seven years, I called a colleague to let him know I was leaving. He never called back. When I got a terrific job in New York City, he knew but never dropped me a note. When I returned to Chicago and was made CEO of a profit center, I didn't hear a word from him. When I got cancer and thought I might die, I got silence from him. When I became national president of the CPCU organization and wrote my first book, he still didn't contact me. But when he lost his job, I heard from him instantly: "Hi, Don. I heard you were back in town. I just wanted to call and say hello. By the way, do you have any jobs?"

I worked next to this guy for years. I had not heard from him in seven years. And now he was calling. No Belt.

Another No Belt called to ask if I could help him find a new job. I did. I called in a favor or two and called him back a few days later to tell him about the interview I had arranged. No answer. I left a message but never heard from him again. I learned later, from someone else, that he had found a different job. But eventually he *did* call—the day he lost that job. No Belt.

Networking goes two ways. You can't just call on people when you need their help. You need to call in good times and bad. The real secret is that you need to actually care about the people in your network. If they know you care, you are golden.

There's one other kind of No Belt networker. They network within a group of people just like themselves. I will give you an example. I know people who connect with only people of their age, color, beliefs, backgrounds, social strata, and discipline—claim adjusters who network with only other claim adjusters, bankers who know only bankers. Black people who network with only black people. White people who network with only white people. No Belts, every one of them.

Networks need diversity and new members if they are going to be robust. When you get to be my age, if you haven't been taking in new members, you will see your network starting to go away. People quit the business, retire, or die. A network of one is no fun.

I've always tried to treat the people in my network as I would like to be treated. That has worked out well.

Do you want to pull away from yet another slice of the competition pie chart? Become a networking Black Belt. And when you do, you will eventually find that the relationships last longer than your career. One day that will mean a whole lot to you.

"The currency of real networking is not greed, but generosity."
—Keith Ferrazzi

CHAPTER TEN

TURN CHANGE INTO DOLLARS.

*"The man who looks for security, even in the mind, is like a man
who would chop off his limbs in order to have artificial ones
which will give him no pain or trouble."*
—Henry Miller

If you are new to the business world, I am now going to
shock you: Many of the people around you would rather fail
than change.

I know that sounds absurd. But I give you my word that it
is absolutely true. I've seen it over and over—at work and with
my family and my circle of friends.

Have you read the little book *Who Moved My Cheese?* by
Spencer Johnson, MD? If you have not yet had the pleasure,
finish this book and then read it next. Heck, if I was being
honest with you I would say put down this book and read the
cheese book right now. Who Moved My Cheese? is one of the
best books ever written. It is all about change—and the cost
of not changing.

I first witnessed workers' reluctance to change when I was

just starting out in business. Allstate had come up with the fairly reasonable idea of having its underwriters—people who accept or reject risks on behalf of the company—handle both homeowner and automobile policies. I was shocked to learn that the underwriters previously had handled only one or the other type of policy. In my department, commercial insurance, we were required to handle at least a half-dozen types of policies. Here is the point: one senior underwriter, a gentleman of about fifty years of age who had been with the company for nearly thirty years, refused to learn the new type of policy. Refused! He eventually lost his job over this refusal. He chose to fail rather than change. It absolutely blew me away.

Let's move ahead about twenty years into my career. I sat across the desk from the person I most admired at work and told him, as bluntly as I could, that he had to support the new leadership or they were going to fire him. This was a full vice president of the company and one of the sharpest people I have ever met. The new leadership was not evil. They just wanted to take the business in a new direction. They were introducing change. My friend said, "I just cannot do it." It was the end of his career. As W. Edwards Deming wrote, "It is not necessary to change. Survival is not mandatory."

Announce a change agenda at work and watch the place go into paralysis. People will not get back to anything resembling normalcy until they know exactly how the change will affect them. Most of the day is consumed by listening to, repeating or trying to clear up rumors. It is a mess.

One of the biggest gripes you will hear about management is that "They just sprung this on us." That is often true. Few organizations communicate a change agenda well ahead of the actual change. Heck, in most cases, it they did, the place would fall apart. So instead, surprise!

Here is the deal. Change is no surprise. It is what it is. It is the next thing. Change is a constant in business. Fluctuations in the economy, growing competition and technological advances make change a necessity. It happens more often now than it did in the past. It will happen even more frequently in the future.

CHANGE HAPPENS, AND YOU MIGHT AS WELL LET IT BENEFIT YOU

So why not embrace change? Let your competition fall apart when change happens. As for you, change brings gifts in the form of opportunities. If you can keep your head when those around you are losing theirs (thank you, Rudyard Kipling), you'll find gold in that there change.

What do you need to do to benefit from change?

First, anticipate it. Always be thinking about what is going on in your business and what trends will need to be addressed. If you see that sales are dropping, ask yourself, what comes next? Expense reductions come next. If you anticipate change you can better prepare for its arrival.

Second, greet change warmly when it arrives. Listen carefully to the real information that is communicated and listen lightly to the rumor mill. I always say that all rumors are true, that it is just the facts that get screwed up. What I mean is that significant facts, such as the date of the layoff, size of the layoff, and names of those about to be fired are not likely to come to you via the rumor mill. The rumormongers might get it right that there is going to be some kind of a layoff. But that's not a problem for you; you already figured it out.

Third, offer to help with the change. Let your boss know that you will do whatever is needed to make this go smoothly. Heck, your boss is probably just as scared as you and might even want someone he or she can talk to during this time. It will serve you well that you are one of the few people be handling the situation in a businesslike manner.

Fourth, put your head down, get back to work, and do your best work. There may be survivors, so now is not the time to look like a problem child. There is opportunity in chaos. Look for it.

Some of the otherwise strongest people I know completely fall apart during times of change. Be the one who grows stronger during such times. The cheese is on the move, and you need to go with it.

Fifth—and this one is important—protect yourself. No need to be a Pollyanna. Bad things do happen to good people. Freshen your résumé. Read Part Three of this book. Make sure your network is in good operating order. Put out some feelers. Be prepared for whatever comes your way.

Support the change. This will mystify your boss, astound your fellow workers, and set you apart from the rest of the crowd. Remember, you are not in a popularity contest. You are playing to win. Winners support the change that the company—the entity that pays you that nice check every so often—wants to introduce.

Here's what you need to do to support the change:

• Learn as much as you can about the reasons for the

change. Again, go to your boss to learn what you can from him or her. Check out what the press has to say. See what is being said about it on the Internet, even from highly biased sites like SoandSoCompanySucks.com. Become an expert on the facts behind the decisions.

• Find out what is needed from you and do it.

• Look confident, even if you are not. Hey, what is going to happen is going to happen whether you look confident or not. You might as well look good during the tough times. It will be remembered later.

• Avoid getting caught up in the rumors and paralysis. This alone will help you stand out to management.

• Make your boss's life easier, not harder.

And then, what will be will be.

During a long career, you'll go through the fire of change multiple times. If you can embrace change when it comes your way, you will once again move ahead of much of your competition. When you think of the wheel of change remember that it is better to be inside, like a spoke or the hub, than it is to be underneath it as it moves.

Now where did I put my cheese?

"You can avoid ulcers by adapting to the situation:
If you fall in the mud puddle, check your pockets for fish."
—Author unknown

CHAPTER ELEVEN

BE WILLING TO WORK THE HARD PILE.

"Don't find fault, find a remedy."
—Henry Ford

Every company I ever worked for bragged about its people—"the best in the business." After you have worked at a couple of companies you come to understand that it's impossible for *every* company to have the best people in the business.

An old boss of mine, Michael Markman, addressed this paradox for me. The truth of the matter was, he told me, that our business, at that time, had *some* of the best people in the business. Like all companies, we also had some of the worst people and a whole lot more who fit into the middle part of the bell curve—hardworking, average employees. That might not sound inspirational, but it was true.

I bring this up to launch into another way that you can step ahead of the competition. This way requires a good understanding of your competitors and how they work. Let's take a quick look at them.

UNDERSTAND THE WORKFORCE AND YOUR COMPETITION FOR JOBS AT THE TOP

At one end of the bell curve, you have a few unfortunates who never should have been hired, have no hope of ever succeeding, and possibly shouldn't be employed by anyone. This is a small group, probably less than 5 percent. Ignore them the best you can, and fire them if you ever get the chance.

You'll find a huge number of employees right in the middle of the curve. They are the backbone of any company. I love them. They give you a good day's work for a fair amount of pay. It's impossible to get anything done without them. They tend to be about 85 percent loyal, and many are long tenured. Some of them are brilliant. All have some something that keeps them from being your direct competition, such as

- They may not have gone to college.

- They may not want the responsibility of being a manager.

- They may hate to travel.

- They may want others to make the decisions.

- They may feel safer in the middle.

Whatever the reason, they have made a choice. Most are comfortable with that choice. Don't look down on them. They are doing what they believe will make them happy or what their circumstances dictate. In some cases, you will be grateful that a person from this group chose not to compete with you directly. He or she might have won the competition.

The world needs the folks in the middle. Treat them with respect. Give them some recognition. Don't for a second think you can run a business without them.

This brings us to the other end of the curve, the one where your direct competition—the last 5 percent or so of the employee population—is positioned. It just takes a couple of good decisions on your part to distance yourself from the below-par performers and from the great mass in the middle. But it takes a lifetime of hard work and great decisions to move ahead of this final group, your competition.

Remember, it is not good enough to make it to the top 5 percent. True success comes when you get into the top 1 percent. Keep your eye on that prize and don't settle for anything less.

WINNERS NEVER SETTLE

The first hurdle you'll face is "settling." Once you hit a certain degree of success you begin to face some of the toughest decisions of your career. The first decision is whether you are going to settle for what you have or go for what is behind door number three?

When you settle, you sound like this: "Gee, this is a pretty cushy job. I am the big boss of this office. My boss is a thousand miles away and pretty much leaves me alone. My people like me. I like them. I'm making good money. I feel safe in this job, and I know how to do it well. The next step would cause me to have to move to Chicago or New York City. It would also place me under the glaring light of the president of the company, a woman who brings in ten people like me, watches them operate, and eventually gets rid of nine of them. I think I'll stay right here until the day I retire."

Someday you will face the decision of whether or not to settle. I'm not here to tell you how to run your life. I just want you to know that you can do so much more with your life *if* you tune out the siren song of settling.

Settling is not success; it's settling.

If you choose not to settle, you'll have to take on the hard pile. That means you could have to

- Handle the important client who no one else has ever been able to please

- Fire that person who has been a pain in the ass at work for the past thirty years, the one everyone hates and is afraid of crossing

- Stand up to the bully boss and get her to change

- Accept the assignment to run the worst office in the fleet, the one located in Cleveland, the one with the notoriously resigned staff of senior employees, the one that has not made money since the 1990s, the one that has defeated the last three high-potential people sent there to run it; yes, that office

- Find a way to cut expenses by 20 percent.

- Introduce processes and procedures to a culture that has never operated efficiently or with any kind of a routine

- Start a new venture from scratch

- Shut down an old venture

- Take on the necessary, but not-so-glamorous jobs in a company, such as managing the backroom.

WORK THE HARD PILE

The hard pile is where those who refuse to settle go to work every day. If you want your dreams to come true, you will visit the hard pile, that is unless dear old dad owns the company.

You'll be amazed at how many people get a good glimpse of the hard pile and then shy away. These people still think they are on the fast track, but actually they are now relegated to the settled group. They think that although they balked at that Cleveland assignment, the big boss will recognize this as a smart move and eventually will give them the Beverly Hills office to run. I calculate those odds at 2 in 100. They are cooked and just don't want to recognize it. The specter of the hard pile claims the reluctant and delusional settlers.

The hard pile is like a gold mine. It's filled with lots of hard work and prone to cave-ins, but it offers the possibility of fabulous riches.

Let me offer some thoughts on failure. My feeling is that if you have not experienced a failure or two in your career, you have not pushed yourself hard enough. We'll take a look at recovering from failure later, but I want to hit another aspect of failure right now.

People have a picture of failure that they carry around in their head. I don't feel that doing the right thing is failure. Think about that Cleveland office I mentioned earlier. My guess is that one of those high-potential leaders sent to run that office should have called up the boss after about sixty days and said, "Boss, we need to shut this place down now and move the profitable business and the three valuable employees I found here to the Pittsburgh office. Then we need to get rid of the rest of the business, fire the rest of the people, and take a write-down on the expenses in the upcoming quarter. This place cannot and should not be saved!"

Would that be a failure? I don't think so. It sounds like a courageous businessperson making the right decision. Would it be a risky decision? You bet. That's why I call it the hard pile.

I love the hard pile. The hard pile is where we come to succeed. It's where we test ourselves and find out how much courage we can muster. It's a place that few dare visit. Success is found in the hard pile, right under that shaky-looking roof.

"Courage can't see around corners, but goes around them anyway."
—Mignon McLaughlin

CHAPTER TWELVE

GET READY TO BE UNCOMFORTABLE.

*"To the degree we're not living our dreams, our comfort zone
has more control of us than we have over ourselves."*
—Peter McWilliams

This chapter is about taking risks. It's a natural follow-up to the last chapter on professional risks, because now we're going to get personal.

CREATE OPTIONS FOR YOURSELF

Success is much more likely to occur when you give yourself options for success. These options are like at bats in baseball. The more times you go to bat, the more chances you have at getting a hit.

Two points about options and opportunities. First, sometimes you get only one opportunity to move to the next level or to do something extraordinary. Second, the person with the most options for success is often the winner.

A buddy of mine was offered the president's job at one of the entities our company owned. However, he was told that if he took the job the entity was going to be sold and he would go with the sale. He had twenty years with the company, loved his current job and had never moved. The new job would require him to move and to leave the company. By the way, there was no guarantee that the new owners would keep him. And the door would not be open for him to return to our company. He had a decision to make, a very difficult decision.

He had always wanted to be president of a company. He thought that at the very least there would be money to be made in the transaction. He felt he was the right person to get the job done correctly. He also guessed correctly that his old company was giving him a subtle hint that his days of advancement were over. He took the job—and took a risk.

It turned out he was really good at the new job. He held it for over a decade. He eventually became chairman as well as CEO. I tried to piece together how much money he had made and quit counting at $25 million. I think it's safe to say that he reached one of his grand goals in life. Good for him. I'm proud of him.

For every person I know like him, I know ten who would have turned down the offer. They would have turned it down even if they knew it was the end of their rise up the ladder. And worse, unless they are pried out of their current jobs, they will hang around, unfulfilled, until retirement. They have settled, and they are not too damn happy about it.

Here comes the killer—brace yourself:

YOU WILL HAVE TO MOVE TO BE COMPLETELY SUCCESSFUL

Hold it. Don't close the book now. Give me a chance to make my case.

What are the chances you will continue moving up the ladder for the forty years or so you may have left in your career and each promotion or opportunity will be located in your current hometown? I'd say about zero point zero (quoting Dean Wormer from *Animal House*).

Who has more chances for success, the woman who won't move and is stuck trying to get promoted at one of the two companies in her area that have jobs in her field, or the women who is willing to relocate to any of the two thousand other companies around the world that have jobs in her field?

A willingness to relocate often gives people a chance to succeed, while a refusal to move can causes them to settle, whether they want to or not. I've seen it happen year after year.

I was born and grew up near the beach in Southern California. I love to surf and to be in the ocean. I love the great weather in Southern California. It lets me be outdoors year round, to run, play golf and take pictures—all things I love to do. Most of my relatives live there, and some could benefit from my living near them. Most of my oldest friends (and at this point in my life the word "old" is quite appropriate) live in California. I, however, live in Chicago, where it is snowing as I type this chapter.

I managed to make it to age thirty-five before I got my first opportunity to relocate. I went from the comfort of my family and surroundings to the frozen tundra of Chicago. My family—my wife and two kids—went with me. We didn't want to move. However, we wanted the success that was possible with this move.

Ten months later we were relocated to Pittsburgh. I had never been to Pittsburgh. I knew not one person in that city. I was transferred to another part of the company that was made up of new people—outsiders who did not share my love of the mother company.

The company sent us to Pittsburgh to scout it out before I had to accept the job. My wife and I rented a car. We were lost for eight straight hours. It's kind of difficult to get around Pittsburgh if you've never been there. We didn't see the sun all day and read somewhere that Pittsburgh had the second-least amount of sunshine of any U.S. city. We never found the suburbs. All we saw was a decaying (this was in the early 1980s) post-industrial city. We fought with each other all day long. We were very happy to get on the plane and fly back home.

The next day, I took the job.

Pittsburgh was just one of the stops on my road to the success I have enjoyed in my life. And here is the oddest part of the deal: we loved Pittsburgh. Great people. Great food. Wonderful golf. And a new and exciting work environment.

Successful people go to Pittsburgh—or to Cleveland—or to wherever the opportunity surfaces.

I've heard every known excuse for not moving. They generally fall into two categories: "I have family here and just can't move," or "My spouse has a career here and I have to be considerate of it."

You're not going to want to hear this, but both of these are excuses for refusing to do the difficult thing that must be done if you are going to give yourself every option for success.

I have family too. What I found is that the phone, the airlines, the iChat on my computer, and e-mail lets me keep in great contact with my family. I make a good effort to stay in touch with family and friends wherever they are on this planet. It's up to me to do this because I am the one who moved. I accepted that responsibility. The airlines love me. I've bought lots of tickets.

I also found that there are a lot of great places to live in this world. Although I took a shot at moving to Japan, all of my moves thus far have been within the United States. We lived in Southern California, Northern California, Chicago (three times), Pittsburgh, Baltimore, and New York City. We loved all of these places. Moving has enriched our lives far more than I could have imagined.

How do you know you can't make it work until you try it? You can always move back home. Don't let your career come up short because you were—I am sorry to use this word—*afraid* to move. Give yourself the options that will allow you to fulfill your grand goals.

As for the spouse's equally important career, I understand that this is tricky business. However, there are opportunities for him or her where you are going. Ask whoever is making you the offer to help you overcome this obstacle. If the company wants you, it will do all it can to help your spouse find a suitable opportunity in the new place. A quote by Confucius that I love speaks to this issue: *"Man who waits for roast duck to fly into mouth must wait very long time."*

Enough said about moving. Let's move on to other ways to create additional options for yourself.

EDUCATION OPENS DOORS

Education is the most obvious way to give yourself more options. When I started out, having a college education was the price of admission. Later on you needed an MBA if you wanted to maximize your chances of making it to the top. At one point in my last few years in Corporate America I worked for a woman who had a PhD, and her boss had a PhD. I am wondering if the cheese has moved again. Do people today need a doctorate to maximize their opportunities?

Having a quality education creates more options for you. Can you get by without one? Sure. There will always be stories of people achieving great success without ever making it out of high school. Will you have more chances for success with a great education? Certainly. Please, at least get a master's degree, even if it takes you five years of going to night school. More education equals more opportunities for success.

AN OPEN MIND CREATES OPPORTUNITIES

Another way to create more "at bats" for yourself is to erase your existing set of "I won't"s. What do I mean by "I won't"?

I won't work for that guy.

I won't work for a woman or for that woman.

I won't work in the sales side of the business.

I won't ever make a lateral move.

I won't work in New York City. (This one is part of a larger limiter that says, "I won't live in New York City, the South, Los Angeles or overseas." The list usually is expanded to include wherever you were just offered a job away from your home turf.)

I won't travel while my kids are still playing soccer.

I won't take a job that requires me to wear a tie.

I won't shave my beard for anyone.

I won't go through life without that keen facial tattoo that I have wanted since I was a kid.

Every "won't" eliminates some possibilities. Be careful with your won'ts. And while you are at it, erase your "can't"s:

I can't speak in public.

I can't fire people.

I can't manage the people who hired me in this business.

I can't learn to do spreadsheets.

I can't put myself in a position where people will say things about me behind my back.

Of course you can. Winners attack their can'ts and overcome them. Those who can have more options.

Here are few more ways to greatly expand your own options:

- Think global rather than local.

- Think about your core skills rather than your technical expertise. If your core skills include leadership, great communication skills, and the ability to negotiate, just to pick a few, you can easily succeed in a job outside of your current department.

- Look outside of work for ways to gain the experience you will need to succeed at work. If you're not getting a chance to build your presentation skills at work, get involved in a charitable organization and build your skills there.

- Seek out opportunity rather than waiting for it to fly into your mouth, as Confucius said.

The most successful people I know all got that way by taking risks. Some of those risks were corporate risks. Other risks were much more personal. No risk, no success.

You can't know for sure whether you will like or dislike something unless you try it. This holds true for almost everything except sticking a screwdriver in a wall socket. Don't try that. Trust me that you won't like it.

> *"Yes, risk-taking is inherently failure-prone.*
> *Otherwise, it would be called sure-thing-taking."*
> —Tim McMahon

PART THREE

"FAIL" WELL

THIS IS WHERE WE EXPLORE WAYS TO DEAL WITH THE UPS AND DOWNS OF YOUR CAREER

Stick around long enough and you will take a beating or two in your career. It doesn't matter if you are trying to hide out somewhere in the middle of the pack or taking risks every day. Somewhere along the line, you screw up, the economy or your company screws up, or you just plain get screwed (that is a technical term for being treated unfairly). Stuff happens.

For the first five years of my career I was full of both ego and naïveté. Now that's a dangerous combination. I remember when our regional vice president called us all together and announced that he had just returned from the home office and had learned that there weren't going to be any layoffs. My first thought was, "Why would he even say such a thing? I thought we were doing great."

Well, we were not doing great. The economy was in a downturn. Competition had put a squeeze on profit margins. The top line had slowed, and the bottom line had deteriorated. Who knew? I certainly didn't know about any of this. My periscope was not up. My boss hadn't mentioned any of this to me, or perhaps I wasn't listening. Apparently I had just missed being canned and didn't have a clue it might have been coming.

Good people get fired all the time in business. Great people get caught in the wrong place at the wrong time, and the ax falls on them. High performance is often an insulator from being downsized (nice word for being canned) but not always. Sometimes whole plants or offices are shut down, with no offers for anyone there to continue on with the company in another location or another role. As I said, stuff happens.

And then there is the dreaded screw-up. Each of us has at least one big screw-up in us. Surviving a major screw-up is one of the challenges we will look at in this section.

We will also look at dealing with a horrible boss; handling the times when you lose your focus, drive, or nerve; and establishing a game plan for getting a new job should the one you have suddenly become "unavailable."

Don't need any of this right now? Great. I suggest that you read it anyway so you can provide some help to those in your network who do need this kind of help. And hold on to the book. You will need it someday.

CHAPTER THIRTEEN

EVERYONE GETS ONE
GOOD SCREWING.

*"Expecting the world to treat you fairly because you are
a good person is a little like expecting the bull not
to attack you because you are a vegetarian."*
—Dennis Wholey

The title of this chapter and the inclusion of the above quote
might keep me from getting the motivational man of the year
award. No problem. I've been screwed before.

I loved working for a living. I loved Corporate America.
I was treated fairly and rewarded well all along the way. I
am now retired from that part of my life, with nothing but
good feelings and appreciation for forty years of continuous
employment.

I did get screwed a couple of times. My guess is that you
will too.

Before I describe the screwings from my own career, I
need to say that, quite often, the screwing is in the eye of the

beholder. Every time I got screwed at work, it made someone else happy. And many of the people around me didn't consider what happened to me a screwing at all. They, of course, were wrong.

I got my first screwing from President Nixon. (And I was not alone.)

In August 1971, I was making less than $9,000 a year. That's horrible money now. Heck, it was horrible money then. At the beginning of August, I was given a nice raise, to be effective September 1. I needed that raise because inflation had grown to 4 percent, my wife was still in college, and we were quite broke. On August 15, 1971 (not that I remember such details), President Nixon imposed price and wage freezes. My raise was out the window. The raise my buddy got the month before? He got to keep it. Screwing number one.

Screwing number two was also going to come in the 1970s, again because of government actions. It was something called Affirmative Action. The big boss, a really old-fashioned Southerner, told me I would be passed over for promotions in the days and weeks ahead because I was male and white.

That screwing never happened. In fact, I have always thought that Affirmative Action was both right and a help to me. It kept me focused on being the best that I could be so that nothing could get in the way of my success.

OK, technically not a screwing, but a pretty interesting look into how things were in America not that long ago.

The real screwings at work fell into two categories: someone less talented than me got the big promotion and I got the big screwing, or just as I was about to hit it big at work, the rug was pulled out from under the business.

In my business the latter usually meant that a huge hurricane hit somewhere on the East Coast or Gulf Coast, the earth moved in California, or fires swept across the land. It was kind of hard to find anyone sympathetic to my plight when actual lives were lost and people's financial lives were ruined. Nonetheless, being screwed by circumstance feels just as bad as being screwed by a misguided boss.

Probably the screwing that hurt the most was the one that happened when I was sure I was finally going to make "officer" for the first time in my career. My boss loved me. I was next in line and well qualified. What could go wrong? Well, I never did find out what went wrong, but something certainly did go very wrong. Another guy got the job. What's worse, I was asked to write the press release. I did. It wasn't my best work.

Stick around long enough and you too will get screwed. The company you devoted your life to will get sold out from under you. Your godfather at work will quit/die/be fired or otherwise leave you high and dry. The company will go into bankruptcy and turn your pension over to the government. On the day there's exciting news to communicate, you will be sent to New Jersey to make the announcement while the women in the next office over will get the trip to Paris. Oh, the screwings never stop.

STUFF HAPPENS. GET OVER IT.

Now that I have vented about the thinly veiled screwings from my life, it's time to offer you some good advice. The advice is this: get over it. Stuff does happen in a long career. Think of the rule that says you will lose your wallet or purse three times in a lifetime. If you know that it's going to happen, when it does, you can react as though it was expected and move on. That's one less loss of a wallet that I will have to put up with in this lifetime. As Helen Keller wrote, "When one door closes, another opens. But we often look so regretfully upon the closed door that we don't see the one that has opened for us."

Bad things will happen to you along the way. You will be too close to the situation to fairly judge whether the decisions behind those bad things are actually the best decisions or in someway will be good for you in the long run. No matter. It's the hurt and the feeling of unfairness that derails many an achiever.

Take your occasional beating. Let it strengthen your resolve. You don't have to win everything today. Tomorrow might even be a better day for winning. And when you get older, take a moment to reflect on the screwings that came your way and write a nice book about them. I did, and I am feeling better already.

> *"And this too shall pass ..."*
> —Attributed to Abraham Lincoln

CHAPTER FOURTEEN

AND EVERYONE GETS AT LEAST ONE HORRIBLE BOSS.

"So much of what we call management consists of making it difficult for people to work."
—Peter Drucker

In the course of a long career you will have many bosses. In fact, on your first day on the job you may have many bosses. Many firms today have some form of matrix management. This can mean you report to several bosses at once—one for your regular work, another for a special project, and still another as your department's representative on the coveted safety committee. On your first day on the job you're likely to end up with that safety committee assignment. It comes with a nifty hard hat and a handy whistle.

Not all bosses are created equal. In fact, there are three kinds of bosses: the "Oh, thank God I have you as my boss" boss, the "Mr. or Ms. Average" boss, and the "Boss from Hell."

Let's look at the Boss from Hell first. This type of boss is so much more interesting than the rest.

You get about three Bosses from Hell in a lifetime of work. They are obstacles who must be overcome. Don't let them drive you out of the company or make you give up on your dreams. Survive them.

Here's how you recognize a Boss from Hell. He or she

- Yells at people

- Makes you look bad in front of other people

- Laughs at your dreams (though most of the time, the Boss from Hell doesn't want to hear anything about your dreams)

- Won't communicate to you or to your team

- Has one person who is his or her favorite (Let's call this person "The Weasel")

- Constantly puts you in your place and tries to make you cower

- Lies

- Makes it impossible for you to win in your job

- Never tells anyone how good you are because he or she wants to hold on to you for selfish reasons

- Doesn't listen

- Doesn't care about and is probably completely unaware of his or her impact on others.

Bad bosses are toxic human beings. You will have a few. You can and must survive them all.

I've had a few bad bosses.

There was the guy who did everything he could to intimidate me from day one. He tried to knock me off balance in my first ten minutes on the job and then tried again each and every day. He was a bully and a coward. I was convinced he was constantly trying to build a case to get me fired.

He didn't care if I was great at my job. I was a threat to him. I wouldn't take his bullying. I threatened to quit and go to the president of our division and tell him why I was leaving. And, I am embarrassed to admit, he and I got into a shoving match in his office on my first day of working for him. He shoved me first—and shoved me hard. Still, getting physical at work should always be a 100 percent no-no. It was not my brightest moment. I'm still ashamed that I took the bait and sank to his level.

I had another boss who never spoke to me or to anyone else who worked for him. He closed the door to his office, turned his back to the window, and didn't listen to the knocks at the door or the phone that was ringing. All day, he played with *Star Wars* toys in his office or talked on the phone, to people I never met. When he did return a message it was always at 3:00 a.m. and in the form of an e-mail or voicemail. This guy not only made me feel as though I was not part of the team, he made me feel as if there was no team. Thank God he eventually quit. By the way, just so you know that life is not always fair, I read that this bozo is currently making well over a two million a year at another company. I may have mentioned this earlier in the book, but the fact that this guy can make so much money while being such a horrible manager and leader just completely blows my mind.

And then there was the totally incompetent boss. This guy was nice enough. He was very well connected politically within the company. Somehow he ended up as my boss and didn't know a thing about our area, nor did he know how to manage people. How did he survive long enough to make it to the ranks of a Boss from Hell? Simple. He lied. He lied at every meeting. He lied to his boss when every other person in the room knew he was lying. He embarrassed us all. He also created a moral and ethical dilemma for his staff: We wondered whether we should tell his boss that he was totally incompetent and a liar.

This boss did one other thing that made him eligible for the Bosses from Hell Hall of Fame. Years later when I got his job, the head of HR told me that I was the only person ever to get promoted to a department head job after turning down a promotion to the home office. I told him he was wrong, that I had never been offered a promotion to the home office. He showed me my personnel file. Sure enough, there was the offer, and there was my signature declining the offer. The problem is I had never seen the offer before, and I never signed it. The Boss from Hell did. He needed me to run things for him while he was playing with his toys, talking on the phone, or going to the movies after lunch. He forged my signature and cost me a heck of a lot of money and opportunity.

SURVIVING A BAD BOSS

So how do you deal with a Boss from Hell?

First things first, if you have a boss that is physically, mentally or sexually harassing you, don't put up with it. Turn him or her in. Talk to a lawyer. Quit if no one steps in to remedy the situation. The longer you stay, the more you will begin to feel that his or her actions are acceptable or, in some perverted way, normal. You will become a victim.

A quick side story: I fired a guy because I had evidence that he was planning to do harm to someone in the workplace. Once he was gone, I asked one of my people to go through his computer and save whatever files needed to be saved. In doing so, we found a rather astonishing collection of pornography and a trail of e-mails that set my hair on fire. He had been sexually harassing every woman who worked for him.

I immediately got human resources involved, and we met with the women. As soon as I closed the door and told them why I was there, they all burst out crying. Each one thanked me for firing the guy. I didn't feel I should be thanked. I felt I should be publicly hanged for having been so oblivious.

I asked them why they didn't speak up. They told me that they had been friends with him long before he was their boss, that he had started off with some mildly off-color jokes, and that they never objected to them. Over time, the jokes become really obscene. The situation grew worse and worse. Somehow, they began to feel guilty. And as the guy grew darker and darker in his actions, they became afraid of him.

The point of the story is that there are evil people out there, and you don't have to put up with them.

You do, however, have to put up with a few Bosses from Hell during the course of a long career. To survive them, you must do one of the following:

- Outlive them. They will be your bosses for only a while. Make the best of it. Put your head down and do your work. Get along the best you can. Pray daily for deliverance.

- Talk with them. Let them know the few things that would really improve your ability to do a great job. Leave the long laundry list of improvements at home. You will be lucky to get one or two things onto the trail of improvement. If you do make progress, continue the effort. If not, see the bullet above.

- Put your requests in writing. Try not to do this one. However, if you run into the following situation, protect yourself. In preparing to write this book I came across a story on the Internet that may or may not be true. The storyteller claims that her boss said, "I *never* said this failure was your fault. What I said was that I was going to blame this failure on you." If you find yourself in that kind of a situation with your boss, put it in writing and keep a copy. You may need it later, when you are asking someone in human resources or personnel to review the circumstances of your firing. Or you may wish to give the documents to the team of lawyers you will need to hire to represent your wrongful termination lawsuit.

• Work quietly to find a better opportunity for yourself within the company. If you can find one that keeps you on track for reaching your goals, by all means, take it. What you don't want to do is let some sorry-ass bastard run you out of the company or derail your successful career. If you let one bad boss run you out of town, you had better buy running shoes. You will continue to run every time you run into another Boss from Hell.

It's funny how life works. Each of my really awful bosses ended up helping me become a success. I learned how to stick it out through difficult times. I learned how to stand up for myself so I could minimize the pain and shorten the time of working for them. I learned I could survive almost any situation if I just kept doing good work and kept my good attitude. I also learned that you need a coach when the going gets tough. Without the help of a couple of great coaches, I might have let the Boss from Hell beat me.

I won't spend much time on the Mr. or Ms. Average Boss. Most of your bosses will fit into this category. Each will have good points and a few flaws. Some will listen to your suggestions on how they can improve. Others will not be mature enough or confident enough to listen to your coaching. They either will harm you or surprise you with their help. Your best tactic is to just do a great job every day and again pray for a great boss to enter your life. That day will come.

When you do get an "Oh thank God I have you as my boss" kind of boss, you are indeed lucky. A great boss, like a great coach or teacher, will advance you at light speed. You will learn new and important things every single day. You will gain new experiences because your terrific boss has the good sense to push you out into the spotlight so you can grow. You will fail a few times and find that you can survive the failures. You will be tested constantly. You will be told the truth about your performance and held accountable for your actions. There will be lots of recognition, not always the kind of recognition you dreamed of, but recognition nonetheless. You will feel important, feel progress, feel respected, and life will be good.

Here is the thing I learned too late. You are with these great bosses for only a short time. They get you promoted, and you are gone. They get new opportunities and move to some other company or some other part of the world. As much as you want them to be there forever, they go. And the worst part is that your next boss could be a Boss from Hell.

GET THE MOST OUT OF WORKING WITH A GREAT BOSS

Don't miss a day working for great bosses. Listen, learn, work hard, and deliver them a great return on their investment in you. Let them know how much you admire, respect, and appreciate them. Let them know for the rest of their lives. Part of what you become when you become successful will be because of them.

I've had a lot of great bosses. My great bosses—Jack Lamm, Eric Thorson, Gary Beyerle, Jim Strohl, Don Shanks,

Bill Henderson, Cathy Buxton, Jack Callahan, Pennington Way III, Frank Patalano, John Amore, Tina Mallie, Michael Markman, Steve Rand, and a number of others—all know that I love them and that I appreciate the investments they made in me.

My Bosses from Hell don't read books, so I won't bother naming them. OK, I will name just one. His name is Asshole. At least, that is what all of us called him. I'll bet you meet him some day on your way to your success.

> *"The survival of the fittest is the ageless law of nature,*
> *but the fittest are rarely the strong. The fittest are those endowed*
> *with the qualifications for adaptation, the ability to accept*
> *the inevitable and conform to the unavoidable,*
> *to harmonize with existing or changing conditions."*
> —Author unknown

CHAPTER FIFTEEN

EVERYONE COMPLETELY SCREWS UP AT LEAST ONE ASSIGNMENT.

"Mistakes are part of the dues one pays for a full life."
—Sophia Loren

My premise here is that you probably will really screw up at least once in your career, survive the experience, and be the better for it—eventually. Winners and successful people survive their mistakes and move on to success.

I've managed to screw up rather spectacularly a couple of times during my forty years in business. Here is a treasury of those screw-ups for you to enjoy or cringe at:

I once agreed to insure a dog grooming business. For reasons I never learned, the shop also sold some very expensive turquoise jewelry. The place was robbed. The jewelry was gone. We had a big loss.

My buddy in the claims department came running over to tell me of the loss. He told me he had proof that this was an inside job, and that I should cancel the policy. Here's where

I made the big mistake. I canceled the policy. I wrote to the agent to explain to him that our claims department felt that the owner was a crook and that the loss was really an inside job. I also mentioned something about the crooked customer lying to us, because we would never have insured the place had we known about the expensive jewelry.

It turned out that the agent's wife owned the store. Selling the jewelry was the agent's idea, and he didn't see any problem with it. And by the way, the agent was one of our company's best.

"Whoops" did not even begin to cover it.

I never did learn who stole the goods. I was too busy trying to apologize to one and all, trying to keep from being sued, and trying to hold on to my job. I can't imagine why I was not fired on the spot. What a really stupid thing to do.

When I went to see my buddy in claims, he had already quit.

This screw-up was no one's fault but mine. I should have insisted on seeing the evidence. I should have been much more tactful in my communications. And I should probably have done a better job of underwriting the policy in the first place.

But I survived to screw up another day.

My next big screw-up. I came in on a weekend to organize the company's library of manuals. I was going to label them properly so we would look professional when the home office audit team showed up on that Monday. They did show up on Monday, just in time to have a laugh at my expense as I learned the hard way that the word manual is spelled m-a-n-u-a-l, not m-a-n-u-e-l. Thanks to my screw-up, we now had the Property Manuel, the Liability Manuel, the Procedures Manuel and so on.

To this day, some of my old friends from my first job still call me Manuel.

Oh, there's more.

I scheduled an offsite meeting at a restaurant. When we arrived, all fifty of us found out that I had mistakenly reserved the restaurant for the next week. It was a very long week before we returned to that restaurant. Can you guess what the major topic of the table talk was that day?

I'm sure I screwed up actual work assignments or missed deadlines. If I did, those experiences must have been so painful that I have purged them from my memory.

I am not alone in the ranks of people who have messed things up big-time. Here are some beauties from those near and dear to me.

Our big boss failed to come home on the evening of his birthday. Too bad, because his entire department, some forty people, were waiting there, along with his family and assorted friends, ready to surprise him. We waited about four hours, until after 11:00 p.m. He never showed. We all went home. Monday was an interesting day. Part of his punishment from his wife was her insistence that he wear a sign around his neck that said, "I am an idiot." We knew that already.

The same guy got very animated in a meeting, accidently stepped into a waste basket, and clanged around the conference room with his foot stuck in the basket while he just kept talking. We all liked that one.

I've had two bosses lean back in their chairs while conducting meetings and go head over heels backwards. I also got to watch the head of a professional organization fall asleep in front of five hundred people and then fall out of his chair, off the dais and into the audience. That perked up an otherwise dull morning.

The screw-ups I want to focus on are the business screw-ups that people make. My favorite involved a colleague and buddy of mine named Dick, who worked for our organization's very powerful zone vice president. Dick solved a long-standing problem that would help my department tremendously. None of us could figure out how he did it. He was so proud of himself that he wouldn't share his solution. He told us he had sold his idea in theory to the big boss. He invited us to fly up to his office to be present for the formal approval.

We flew up to the zone office and arrived in time to see the zone vice president descend the glass stairway like a god coming down from heaven. As he made his grand entrance, I looked over my buddy's paperwork and saw, for the first time, the math that supported his solution to the problem.

I said to Dick, "Shouldn't that decimal place be over one spot?"

As the zone VP said his hellos, my buddy reviewed his math and saw that I was right.

Just then, the zone VP said, "Let me quickly turn the meeting over to Dick. I just got off the phone with the chairman, telling him all about the solution that Dick developed on his own. The chairman was so thrilled that he is, as we speak, sharing the good news with the board of directors. Dick, please show these folks how your created a miracle."

The rest of the meeting did not go very well.

Dick quickly got to the point. Before he told us how he had solved the problem, he told the zone VP that he had made a bit of a math error. The solution wasn't going to cost $10 million. It was going to cost $100 million. Dick asked the zone VP if that would be a problem. Yes, it would be a problem.

Another of my favorite screw-ups involved the purchase of an expert system—software that businesses use to help them make decisions. An executive committed the company to spending millions of dollars to purchase the system. It was very much needed, the executive said, because we were losing money hand over fist in this department. Someone asked about the brains—the fact base that the system ran on. It turned out the brains were based on the expertise of our senior person in this department, the same senior person whose ideas and decisions had cost us so much money over the years. We had just mechanized his failures. Ouch!

Small errors happen. And if you are responsible for them, they can really hurt. My favorite small error happened when a buddy of mine did not proofread his letter to one of our largest clients, the Earhart Lange Sausage Company. His letter began, "Dear Mr. Long Sausage." Enough said about that one.

At some point, *you* are sure to be added to my list of culprits. You will call someone by the wrong name, fail to include an important fact or fail to inform your boss of a problem, thus causing her to be lambasted by her boss for not giving her a heads-up. You will miss a deadline, make a decision that costs the company big money, or hire the wrong person. You will screw up. Careers are long and, given enough opportunity, you will have your very own Manuel moment.

LIFE CONTINUES EVEN AFTER YOU SCREW UP

So what? Who cares? If you make a mistake, admit it, recover as best you can, apologize, and move on. The real mistakes happen when people

- Try to hide or cover up their mistakes—take President Nixon, for example.

- Fail to acknowledge their errors—take almost any president, for example.

- Blame them on someone else. This one gets you nominated to the Creep at Work Hall of Fame. We will find out you did this, and we will get back at you.

If you screw up at work, stand up, admit it, don't make excuses, apologize, take your medicine, and put it behind you. As Tupac said, "Life goes on."

None of the examples of business screw-ups I cited claimed any victims. All of the people who made those mistakes survived them. They all went on to have wonderful careers. So will you. Just do the right things when your day comes.

Want to hear one that was fatal? How about leaving a drunken voicemail rant about how dishonest and stupid the

CEO is—and leaving it on the wrong phone? Whoops, and good-bye.

I asked a boss of mine why he didn't fire one of my peers when he made a bad decision that had cost us about $5 million. My boss said:

> *"Why would we fire him?*
> *We just invested $5 million in his education."*

CHAPTER SIXTEEN

EVERYONE GETS FIRED AT LEAST ONCE.

"You're fired."
—Donald Trump

Not every firing is as succinct and as honest as the way Donald Trump does it. Some "You-are-out-of-here" communications are so poorly done that they're just plain cruel. Whether you're told "You're fired!" or some less-than-direct person from HR tells you that this is all going to work out for the best, you will experience termination at least once. It ain't pleasant. But it is what it is.

Let's just, for one dreadful minute, assume that you just got fired.

YOU'RE FIRED! NOW WHAT?

First, Grab hold of your senses! Your ears will be ringing and your mind will be all over the place as you try to deal with the reality that you have been let go. You need to be listening

very carefully right now. Many "reductions in force" come with
opportunities. But you need to listen for them:

- There may be options such as, leave now and get paid
  a week for every year you have with the company, or
  stay until the end of the year or until the sale is complete and get two weeks for every year.

- You may be able to negotiate a bit. Can I get outplacement? Can I stay until the end of the year? Can
  I get a letter of recommendation? Can you place me
  on a list of those who would like to be rehired? Will
  you pay for the classes I just signed up for at school?
  Now is the time to be thinking and asking—not getting mad or getting rattled.

- I remember one woman who, when I fired her, turned
  her back on me and would not speak another word.
  I don't recall if I got around to mentioning the jobs
  becoming available in another department. My guess
  is I did not.

- The nice HR rep might hint at some things you
  should know. A question such as "Do you have any
  friends in IT?" might be a way of telling you the company is about to do some hiring in IT. But if you aren't
  listening fully, you won't pick up on the hints.

- Make sure you understand your benefits and what
  will happen to them. Make the choices that must be
  made before you leave.

Second, don't lose your mind. This is no time to go to the bar, the casino, or out with all the other folks who just got fired. This is a really good time to go home to your family.

Third, push all those nasty thoughts out of your head. It sounds like fun, but the price is too high to

- Burn your bridges.

- Sabotage the workplace.

- Go to the press and find yourself featured on the six o'clock news talking about how your old company is actually the devil.

Fourth, watch out for the natural things that happen when any of us is fired. Many of these reactions aren't beneficial:

- We deny it is true. We think something will change at the last minute, and someone will come in to save all of us "good guys." The cavalry was also fired. This is going to happen. It's time to deal with it.

- We become a deer in the headlights. We put our lives on hold and don't do much to protect ourselves. Lots of people just wait to finally get crushed. And the crusher is on the way.

- We get angry. At some point in the process we all become angry. I once put my hand through the drywall in my basement. Be aware of your anger. Embrace it in some safe and out-of-the-public place. Don't hurt anyone with it and *do not* hurt yourself. Anger passes quickly, if you let it.

• I have a friend who is still angry about being fired—still angry after a year. He can't have a conversation about it, not even during an interview with a potential employer, without his anger spilling out. I can't tell you his real name. Let's just call him Still Unemployed.

• We panic. By "panic" I mean that some of us will jump at absolutely anything that's offered. Taking a new job for half the pay is a sign of panic. Taking a new job at about the same pay for about the same work, but without the benefit of a company car, that's not panic. That's doing what you need to do.

• We give up. I am always amazed at how many people drop out of the race after a firing. They retire. They change professions. They fall victim to somebody's pitch about starting their own business. The firing knocks the energy right out of them. It happens more than you might suspect.

I was reminded of the pain associated with a firing while watching the HBO program *In Treatment*. The episode was titled "April: Week 7." In it, April, a young cancer patient, was asked by Paul, her psychotherapist, "Did living seem hard before you got sick?" April immediately said, "No." She then thought for a moment and came up with a line that hit me like lightning. "There used to be this path. It was steep, tiring. But it was well lit. It's not there anymore. It is completely gone. Did I just make it all up?"

Paul replied, "No. You just got rerouted. Your life's path just got changed, without your consent."

The reason this hit me so hard is that I have seen this happen to my friends over and over again. Their lives are rerouted by a firing, rerouted without their consent. And in many cases, they never get over it.

RECOVERING FROM HAVING YOUR LIFE RE-ROUTED WITHOUT YOUR CONSENT

If you find yourself in this kind of a situation, recognize it and deal with it. Work quickly through the anger and sense of loss and start looking for a new path. The path is out there, I promise you. It is exceptionally hard not to take the firing personally. In most cases, it is just business and just the way it is. That sucks, but life goes on. Better days, success, and happiness are still ahead.

Firings at work often are like clearing the underbrush in the forest. It needs to be done periodically for the good of the organization. The organization will eventually be better off for the event. But you will need a plan to move on with your life.

Here's a simple plan for getting a new job:

1. Look around you.

See if the company downsizing you has other jobs available that would suit you and for which you are well qualified. One of the biggest downsizing events of my career caused us to fire 1,500 people. At the end of the firing week I checked with HR. They had 350 jobs open. It's worth checking out.

2. Work the network.

We are all in this together. Let people know that you are available. Let them know that you would appreciate their keeping their eyes and ears open for you.

3. If your company has outplacement, take full advantage of it.

Some companies offer outplacement services to some or all of the people they downsize. This basically gives you an office to go to, a coach to help you with your transition, a support team of people to help you find the next gig, office supplies and machines like fax machines and copiers, résumé writing assistance, a library of resources for helping you find those who might need your services, and someone who will push you to take on this challenge as if it were an actual job. I love outplacement companies. Use them if you can.

4. Check out company websites.

Most companies list open jobs on their websites. Unfortunately, many of these sites are not updated on a regular basis and are hard to navigate and hard to use. They often offer no easy way to contact a real human being. Nevertheless, use these sites as best you can.

5. Check out the biggest job services, like Monster. com.

There is a whole game plan for conducting Internet job searches. You have to use keywords and a whole bunch of stuff I am not qualified to tell you about. Find someone who is an expert in this area and follow his or her advice. Companies like Monster didn't get to be huge by not getting people jobs. Give them a try.

6. Check back.

Just because your old company or some other company you are interested in has no jobs available today, that's no reason for you not to check back in a month. Things change. Don't ever scratch a potential employer off your list.

It's the same story for your network. Call them about once a month to keep them posted on your status.

7. Read the papers.

If you read that a company in your industry just started a new niche by hiring an entire team away from a competitor, call both companies. Either or both might have opportunities for you. Don't wait to see what happens. Act quickly.

8. Go sit on a rock and find ways to expand your search.

Take time to get a way for a few days to think about how you can generate more possibilities. Have you just been looking in your own city, just looking at large companies, restricting your search to managerial rather than technical jobs? Time to think bigger.

You might also think wider than your current industry. I always thought my experience as an insurance underwriter would translate well to the world of banking, mergers and acquisitions, or investment research or to something like working for the FBI. I also thought about teaching, or being a trainer, or a consultant. Widen your thinking and improve your odds.

And now for a bit of the world according to Don. I do not believe that your or my self-worth is tied up in any one thing. We can do new things with our lives. The ability to adapt and to be flexible is inside each of us. If the light on our path is extinguished, it is up to us to seek a new light and a new path. It may be steep and tiring, but it will take us to a place *we choose* to go. If we just give up and declare the path lost, boredom, depression, and anger will come along to lead us their way.

9. Count on your coach.

You need someone to lean on during times of transition. If you have a coach, great. If you don't, find someone. Ideally this will be a friend who is upbeat and willing to help you stay positive throughout this experience. Job searches without any outside support are often nightmares. Get all the help you can get. Don't go it alone.

10. If you have no luck, change something.

I know one guy who always uses me as a reference. The problem is I tend to tell people the truth. I am always happy to tell his prospective employers about his good points. However, when they ask me point-blank questions such as, "Would you hire this guy to run an office filled with difficult-to-manage people?" I am likely to say, "Heck, no. He always has problems with difficult people."

If you are using several people as your references and you are not getting the jobs, change the people on your list.

If your résumé is not attracting interest, prepare a new one.

Ask the executive recruiter you are using to give you some honest feedback. Unless you ask, he or she may never tell you.

And lastly, is there something that no one is telling you that has cost you opportunity after opportunity, some blind spot you have? Is your breath bad enough to remove makeup from twenty-five feet? Do you close your eyes when you talk to people? Do you get too close to people and invade their personal space, like an old friend of mine who insists on telling me stories while his face is no more than a foot from my face *and* he is smoking a cigarette? Is someone in the industry actively poisoning the pond for you? Do you talk too much or too little? Where is that coach of yours? You need the truth, and you need it right now. You can't fix what you don't know.

The aforementioned steps should keep a job seeker pointed in a positive direction.

A couple of other thoughts:

This is a bad time to be going on that vacation of a lifetime. You need to conserve your cash and to be around town, taking on this transition as though it is real work, because it is. If you normally take no more than two weeks a year of vacation, take two weeks. Do not take two months, or the summer, or golf season. Get that job now.

If you think you're about to land a job, keep looking anyway. Some of my biggest heartaches have been delivered by companies that were going to hire me, told me so, and then never contacted me again. Until you have signed the deal, you are still in the job market.

Once you get a new job, thank people. I have, on two occasions, sent people flowers for the help they gave me in getting a new job. Let people know your new contact information, tell them something about the new gig and thank them for their help, whether their help got you the job or not.

One last thing:

You are a valuable human being.

Your value is not tied to a job. You are valuable because you are a son, daughter, parent, neighbor, or friend. You are valuable because of your contributions in the past and in the future. You are valuable to God. You are valuable to me. You count as a human being.

Don't let a transition period get your goat. This too shall pass. There is no shame in it. It is what it is. Work the plan and work it hard. Good things will happen.

Let's hope you don't ever need any of this chapter's information. However, if you have a friend who needs some help along the way, point him or her toward this chapter. We are all in this together.

"You're hired."
—Donald Trump

CHAPTER SEVENTEEN

EVERYONE NEEDS SOME "BOUNCE BACK" IN THEM.

"The strongest oak of the forest is not the one that is protected from the storm and hidden from the sun. It's the one that stands in the open where it is compelled to struggle for its existence against the winds and rains and the scorching sun."
—Napoleon Hill

If you're just starting out in your career, it's hard for you to imagine how long it will last. Careers seem to go on forever, and then they are over in a flash. Here is what I know from my long career: You will be up. You will be down. Your energy level will be tested. Negative events will pile up on you one after another, just when you least expect them. Your ability to get up, go to work, put a smile on your face and exude confidence and a good attitude day after day, year after year, that will be tested as well.

One of the most touching moments of my career came at a dinner we threw for the failed leader of our company. He had been forced to quit. The press and stockholders ran him out of his decades-long career at the pointy end of a stick. His last days were spent listening to angry people tell him he was an awful person. Like I said, we will all have our ups and downs, and his "down" was as down as it gets.

My boss decided we should throw our chairman a small party to honor him and his wife. He didn't do this as a business gesture. He did it to honor a fellow human being who had stood with us in the trenches for many, many years.

Toward the end of the party, each of us got up to tell the honoree what he had meant to us in our careers. Nice touch, but pretty standard stuff. At the very end, his wife got up and said, "I've never spoken at a company event. If you don't mind, I want to tell you what it has been like to be the wife of the chairman when the wind was no longer behind the sails."

At that, she stepped behind her husband, who was seated. She put her hands on his shoulders for support. She spoke from her heart, with no notes of any kind. She told us how he would get up each morning, put on his best suit, select a lively looking tie, and make sure his shoes were shined and his shirt was pressed. He would sit down for a cup of coffee with her and tell her the things he planned to do that day to turn the ship around. He would smile, kiss her, and head off to the battle. He repeated this every single day until the end. At age 60-plus, and with the weight of the world on him each day, the chairman found the inner strength to keep on going into battle with the mind-set that "Today will be the day we turn it around."

As she told the story, tears ran down her face. Tears ran down the chairman's face and down each of our faces. It was the single coolest thing I've ever seen a spouse do for her partner. I will never forget it.

The story begs two questions: Where did the chairman's energy and optimistic attitude come from? And, How can I get some of that?

I also might ask how you get a partner like the chairman's wife, but I already have such a partner, my wife, Linda.

A long career, especially when you work hard and have high expectations of success, will test your inner resources.

I mentioned earlier that I feel like I have been plugged into a wall socket all my life. Most of my energy comes effortlessly, if not naturally. I don't know if it is from my parents, my love for winning, the candy I eat (and shouldn't), the coffee I drink in excess, my daily running, or from the inner bottomless pool of bullshit that is truly at the core of me. It may be a combination of all of the above. Whatever it is, it sure makes my life worth living.

Put me in the confessional and I will tell you that I have

- Been worn out or burned out at work

- Been discouraged to the point of tears

- Thought about settling

- Thought about quitting

- Self-medicated with Scotch, wine, and beer, but thankfully gave that up completely twenty years ago

- Lost my sense of humor for a time

- Showed anger

- Become resigned at times

I don't know anyone who can make it all the way to the finish line without having some of those same down moments. We are human. Our inner resources do run down from time to time.

Let me add a side story: In my fifties I ran the Pikes Peak Marathon. This is a 26.2-mile marathon that starts at 6,500 feet altitude and goes to the top of Pikes Peak, which is at 14,110 feet—not that I was counting. It was eighty-five degrees at the bottom of the mountain and fifteen degrees and snowing at the summit. And once you got to the top, you had to turn right around and run down the mountain to the finish. You didn't get to run on the nice road that goes up the mountain. Instead you ran a goat path called the Barr Trail, a scary, twisting, root- and rock-filled path that hangs on the side of the mountain like rope.

When I reached 13,000 feet, I had just about had it. I came across a race official sitting on a rock and asked him what my options were. He said, "You can continue on another hour or so to the top, get to see the top of the mountain, and get a ride back to town with all the other losers. Or you can turn around here and run or walk back down the mountain, in which case you will have run twenty-two miles for absolutely nothing. Or I can call in a helicopter that you can meet in that meadow down there, and they will have you back to town in ten minutes, lighter by the several hundred dollars they charge for that service. Or you can man up, point your feet up the mountain, go to the top, turn around and finish what your started. It's up to you."

Well, if you put it like that.

I pulled myself back up and finished the race. I am proud of that finish to this day.

LEARN TO PULL YOURSELF UP

You will get knocked down, tired, discouraged, and worn out in your career, and you will have to pull yourself up. Here are some ways to do that:

Get a coach.
Sorry to keep bringing up the coach, but a coach can serve the same purpose as that race official. A coach will spot your flagging energy or attitude and work with you to help you recover.

Have an outlet for your frustration.
Mine has always been running. If I tell you I am losing weight and preparing for a marathon, you can interpret that to mean, "I am really frustrated at work, and I'll be damned if I am going to let it get the best of me." I run, therefore I do not strangle.

The bar is not an outlet; it is an escape.

Hang around positive people.
If your best friend at work hates her job and hates your boss, it is not going to work out well for you. Find people who want to win and stick with them.

Find a way to rejuvenate yourself.

Now I am going to reveal my most selfish act. For all the years I worked, I took a one-week vacation each year by myself. I didn't bring along my wife, my kids, my golfing buddies, or anyone. I took my surfboard and went to Hawaii. I surfed all day, every day. On Sunday, I went to the Pro Bowl—I always timed the trip so that I could go to the Pro Bowl. The next day I returned home. I did this for a couple decades.

I also had a hideaway that I could go to if I was just completely burned out and could not make it through another day. The hideaway was the Buccaneer Resort in St. Croix, Virgin Islands. When I first started going there, the resort had no phones, no newspapers and no television. You could get in a week's worth of rest in only four days, or so it felt.

Selfish? Absolutely. Necessary? It was for me. I needed those moments to rejuvenate myself and to keep me charged up for the long run. My family supported me, or at least never complained. It kept me from running out of fuel, and it always gave me something to look forward to.

One of my terrific bosses, Penn Way, helped rejuvenate his team in another way, shortly after a fortysomething colleague of ours had died of a heart attack. He was not the first of our teammates to die early at the pressure cooker we called work, located in the financial district of New York City. Penn asked us how we were feeling. Several of us offered up that we were fried. He told us to come back to his office at 2:00 p.m.

When we returned, he told us he had arranged for all of us to go to Canyon Ranch to rejuvenate for a few days. Canyon

Ranch is one of the finest spas in the world. We ate right, walked, ran, did other exercise, and got massages and other spa treatments every day we were there. We laughed at every meal. We never talked business. It probably extended our life and made us fit to fight another day. Thanks, Penn.

What is your plan to rejuvenate yourself? You will need one. You need to think about it a little selfishly. As much as I love my wife and my kids, driving off to Disney World with a carload of family would not rejuvenate me. I did lots of vacations like the Disney trips. Fun? Yes. Good family time? Yes. Rejuvenating? Not for me.

Lots of people use religion or meditation to help them rejuvenate. If that works for you, great. Find something that will renew you.

Have a life outside of work.

I don't mean that you should be a businesswoman or businessman by day and a doughnut-maker by night. What I mean is that you need something that takes you away from the office each day. For most of us that is family. For others it's volunteer work. Some play an instrument in an orchestra. You need something that makes you put down the briefcase and turn off the BlackBerry every now and again.

I found out what having no other life was like when I worked in New York City. I lived two buildings over from the office. We owned no car. Our kids had moved on to college and adult life. We rented an apartment, so we had no home maintenance to-do list for the weekends. And the apartment was so small that neither one of us wanted to spend much time in it. My wife shopped, traveled and hung out with friends. I just worked 24/7. No life, just work. It took me about eighteen months before I could take it no longer and moved on to another job in another city. As much as I love work, and loved the work I did in NYC, I needed another life, as well.

Learn to say no.

When you are a winner, when you get things done, people will constantly ask you to join them for this project or that committee. You will want to say yes to all of these requests. But when you are feeling a bit overworked—run ragged—it is time to say no. Never let your commitments overwhelm you. Take full control of your life.

Study resilience.

There are books about resilience, seminars on the subject, and gurus who, for a fee, will coach you about resilience. If this is an area where you need to improve, seek knowledge. Seek help.

You have to be a bit selfish if you want to be able to perform at a high level over a very long period of time. You are the key to your own survival.

"People are like stained-glass windows. They sparkle and shine when the sun is out, but when the darkness sets in, their beauty is revealed only if there is a light from within."
—Elisabeth Kübler-Ross

CHAPTER EIGHTEEN

EVERYONE NEEDS TO BE ABLE TO DETERMINE "UP" FROM "DOWN".

*"Without measurement, the unfortunate outcome is
the failure to meet strategic goals."*
—Eric Kurjan

We humans do some interesting things. For example, some of us make absolutely no career progress for a very long time. And as long as we can pay our bills, we kid ourselves into believing that we are doing just fine. If your grand goal in life is just to be able to pay the bills, you're doing just fine. Most of us have larger goals.

We need to be seriously honest with ourselves if we are to find success in the size we seek. We need to be able to determine up from down.

Let's explore the signals we get at work that tell us how things are going.

PERFORMANCE REVIEWS

Performance reviews, those formal meetings in which you sit down with the boss to discuss the progress you are making, have been homogenized with the introduction of templates and performance review software. By "homogenized" I mean that the reviewer often selects wording from drop-down boxes instead of finding his or her own words to describe the work being evaluated. I find that to be a shame. It makes most reviews read pretty much the same. They lack emotional and creative content. On the other hand, these standardized performance reviews at least gives some assurance that some kind of evaluation will take place each year.

If you are lucky enough to get an annual performance review, listen to your boss very carefully. If it's the homogenized review that is so common today, you will not learn much. Still, take it seriously and take the opportunity to sit down with the boss and get some feedback about how you are doing. A well-done review will be a strong indicator of whether you are still on track with your career game plan or if you have temporarily fallen off track.

A couple of more thoughts on the review process:

If you boss notes more than once that you need to improve in a particular area, or if more than one boss notes this, believe it. Even if your mind, your ego, tells you that your boss is hopelessly misguided and grossly unfair, take the recommendation seriously. Explore it. There is likely to be at least a kernel of truth in the assessment. Find out how you can fix the problem. Ask your coach or someone else for help.

By the way, when I read the same assessment over and over again in the "area for improvement" sections of a worker's performance reviews, that assessment is always spot-on. The reason the same comment keeps appearing is because the person being reviewed disagrees with it, has a blind spot about this flaw, does not think it is important enough to fix, or just can't fix it.

To be worthwhile, a review needs to include insightful comments about your specific performance, thoughtful ideas on how to improve or prepare for the next step up the ladder, and sincere recognition for your good work. Otherwise, your boss is doing the review just to get it off of his or her must-do list. Schedule some face time with the boss to at least try to get some meaningful feedback. You need honest feedback to keep moving forward, and your boss is the best person to provide it.

Some people will strongly disagree with this next observation.

You don't need to get the highest possible score on each and every performance review. As a boss, I always dreaded reviewing the few prima donnas who threw absolute fits. I gave them anything lower than the highest possible ranking. I would rate them as "exceeds expectations," and they would wage a battle to get that changed to "significantly exceeds expectations." They were pains in the derriere—and you don't need to pardon my French.

I think I got every significant promotion of my life off of "meets expectations for this position" ratings. A "meets expectations" rating meant that I was doing my job. I might not have had the experience to rate anything higher. I was moving too fast to gain that kind of experience. And the few times I did get rated "significantly exceeds expectations," I found myself going nowhere. I had hit a plateau.

Don't let your ego cloud your vision. Look at what is being said. Consider the signals you are getting. Ignore the rating unless it drops below "meets expectations." If that happens, you are probably in big trouble. Make some changes and get back on track.

By the way, a performance review discussion with your boss is a great place to do a few things:

- Share your career dreams with your boss. Your boss might laugh. He or she might be intimidated by the size of your dream or might ho-hum it. Or you might just find someone who says, "Let me help you get there." That little statement is gold.

- Ask for an investment in your development. This is where you start the process of gaining company support for your MBA, law degree, or such professional designations as CPCU, CLU, or CPA. If the company invests in your future, it's a strong signal that your career is on track.

- Suggest ways that the two of you can work more effectively together. This is where you ask for more communications, more space to operate, and more face time with your boss's boss. All of life is a negotiation. This is a place to practice those skills.

- Agree on some next steps to get you to the next level.
  Or your boss might just shut down the discussion, ask
  you to sign the review, and tell you to get back to work.
  No problem. You have just been "homogenized." Your
  progress and feelings are not as important to the boss
  as is checking off your progress review as "Completed."
  It really didn't have much to do with your progress.
  It was a chore that needed to be done by the boss. It
  happens all the time. Find another time and way to get
  some honest feedback from your boss—and pray that
  he or she matures in job. You really do deserve some
  feedback on a regular basis.

SALARY AND BONUSES

You will find out when you become the boss that salary administration is difficult at best. You are given a salary target that
you can't exceed. If that target works out to 4 percent raises for
everyone, and you give 6 percent to one person, someone else
must get only 2 percent. That's how it works.

Most salary administration doesn't mean much. It gives
you just about enough new money to make up for inflation.
It might advance you economically a small amount. Even if
you do get more than the target, let's say 50 percent more than
the target, it's still not a boatload of money if the target is 4
percent and you get 6 percent.

What becomes important is your ability to spot outliers or
anomalies. It is the odd salary events that should catch your
attention and send you a signal:

- If all of a sudden you get a 10 percent raise, somebody is trying to make sure you're a happy camper.

- If you get a "one-time performance bonus" that comes out of the sky, again, someone is trying to keep you happy.

- If you do get more than the target year after year, you are being looked after.

- If your bonus is near the top of the range, something good is happening.

- If your boss gives you an unexpected grant of stock shares that are restricted and can't be sold for three years, that's great news! The company is trying to hold on to you with golden handcuffs.

- If you get a raise or bonus sooner than expected, such as at six months sooner, that's a good thing.

By the way, these kinds of things rarely happen for anyone who is not considered a high-potential or high-performing employee. If these good things happen to you, smile in the knowledge that others are recognizing your value.

If you get average increases at regular intervals with average bonuses, this is standard fare. It is to be expected. This is what happens to most of us most of the time. It's a signal that things are on track. It's neutral. Don't be crushed by it. Don't be too thrilled with it. Work hard to get into the better scenarios described.

Here is a signal you don't want to miss: If everyone gets a raise and you don't, watch out. This is bad news nearly 100 percent of the time. Either you are being set up to be sent out the door, or your boss is so incompetent and insensitive that he of she has neglected to give you a clear explanation of why you should not worry. If you don't have that explanation, protect yourself. Find out what you need to fix at work, and fix it. You may also want to update your résumé and ping the network. This is serious.

If everyone gets a bonus and you don't, you're also in trouble. At one company I worked for, no one got a chance to miss a second bonus, unless, after you missed that first bonus, the business climate dictated that there would be no bonuses for anyone the next time around. If you missed a bonus that others received, you were on your way out the door. In fact, you were probably in your last ninety days.

A word about bonuses.

There is usually a threshold, target and maximum bonus that you can achieve for any year. The threshold might get you 10 percent of your base salary as a bonus, target might be worth 25 percent, and the maximum could be 50 percent. Events firmly in your control and completely outside your control will determine the size of your bonus.

If you're smart, you will never plan or count on getting one penny of bonus. In my business, the insurance business, we have had otherwise dandy years wiped out in the last week of December, when the earth shook somewhere. Don't ever count on getting a bonus.

When you do earn a bonus, it will never be what you expected. Last-minute decisions by the compensation committee or the work and will of the CEO (sometimes working in your favor and other times not so much) will cause adjustments. You have little ability to do much about these adjustments. The check will show up, its ink will be dry, and it won't bounce. Be happy for any bonus that comes your way.

Over the course of about thirty years of being eligible for bonuses, here is what I learned: In the long run bonuses will equal out to the "target" level. In the short run, you will get a big fat *zero* when you most need the bonus. And every now and again you will get your socks blown off with an obscene amount of money.

Every ten years, add up your bonuses and test me on my theory, that over the long run you will earn the target rate.

By the way, don't look for fairness in bonus schemes. Should they be fair? Of course. Are they fair? Often not. Get over it. You will find that, given enough time, you will sometimes be treated unfairly. At other times you will be almost embarrassed at the riches thrown your way.

Companies send signals with money. If you understand the signals, they will provide you with very valuable feedback about how you are doing.

ASSIGNMENTS

Few signals at work are more clear than the ones sent when assignments are given. Who gets what assignments tells you a lot about people's status.

If you are assigned to a team that will work in secret on the overall reorganization of the company, take that as a strong positive signal. Change is coming, and you will have an opportunity to direct and implement that change.

If you are asked to work as the number-two person for a woman who plans to retire in six months, consider this your screen test. You are being looked at as her probable successor. The job is yours to win or lose.

If you get the assignment to take a paid leave from the company to go work for a local charity, make sure you clean out your office before you leave. You are not coming back.

I use to bug the CEO of our company to give me the job of running one of our overseas companies. One day he took me aside and told me never to ask him again. He said, "Haven't you figured out that no one ever survives that assignment. We send people there at the end of their career so we can cut them loose where no one can see them cry." Now that got my attention. I never asked again.

Look for the signals in your assignments. But not every assignment sends a signal. There is work to be done that is not directly tied to your own career game plan. It's the outliers you need to spot, the juicy assignments that give you visibility up the line. These are the assignments that team you with other high performers—where the CEO is the sponsor of the team or the project. Such assignments are strong and positive signals that things are going well for you.

Landing the assignment that puts you in charge of taking away everyone's company car and monitoring his or her magazine subscriptions, that's not such a good signal.

EXPOSURE

If you're identified as a high-potential worker, you'll find yourself being exposed to all kinds of interesting situations. Here are some of the things you might get to do:

- Meet with key clients or important trading partners

- Travel alongside key executives, where you can get important face time and start to form important relationships

- Attend events that others at your level do not get invited to, such as the annual leadership conference. These kinds of invitations are often disguised as your being asked to "work the event." Yes, you will work. But the real reason to have you there is to start the process or ignite the spark that will lead to your joining that group as a regular member.

- Be included at "insider" events. These are the communication events normally reserved for leaders well above your current position. You are there to observe and learn—a very good signal.

On the other hand, if you are sent out of town every time the CEO comes to visit, if you are kept hidden instead of exposed, that just might be a signal. Not all signals are good.

THE SUCCESS LINE

Every company has an undocumented and hard-to-figure-out Success Line. This is a choreographed, sequential pattern of assignments that leads to the top. All companies are different. There are too many variables to cover in any book. I will give you one example and show you how to spot the Success Line.

One company I worked for had a Success Line that looked like this:

Worker bee → Supervisor → Department Manager → Regional Manager of a small and out-of-the-way office in Rochester, Pittsburgh, Redding, or another underappreciated city > Regional Manager of the flagship office, usually in places such as Chicago, New York City, or Los Angeles → Zone Vice President → President → CEO → Chairman

Only a few exceptional employees were invited onto the Success Line express. Fewer still excelled at each stop along the way. Only one person out of fifty thousand or, if you include all those who came and left during my thirty years with the company, perhaps several hundred thousand made it all the way to the top.

Is there a Success Line at your company? You will have to be a bit of a company historian to spot it. Do you know the work histories of your top leaders? How did they progress through your company? Look for common lines—similar assignments or career moves. Once you spot these similarities, these trends, you can be honest with yourself and determine whether you are on, near to, or a long way from the Success Line. Being on the Success Line is a very positive signal. Being nowhere near it, that too is a signal. Look for the signals.

ASSORTED OTHER SIGNALS

A company I worked for spent something like $60,000 to send me to Harvard to take a course in strategic marketing. Two other guys went with me. One was someone who, I felt, would one day run the entire company. I thought the other guy would run an important profit center for the company. My grand goal was to run the profit center to which I was currently assigned. Coincidence? I don't think so. I took being sent to Harvard as a very strong signal that I was still on track to have my dreams come true.

By the way, the guy I figured would run the company ended up as its president. I'm very proud of him. He is a terrific executive. And the other guy did indeed end up running an important profit center—at another company. I too ended up running an important profit center, but at yet another company. I am proud of all of us.

Having a company decide to invest in your education is a great signal that you are headed for success. Having an executive coach assigned to you is either an outstanding signal or a sign that you are just one false move away from being canned.

I love executive coaches and eagerly accepted the chance to work with them when offered the opportunities. Many of my competitors refused that help. It was their loss and often my gain. However, executive coaches—highly experienced, highly respected, highly paid outside consultants—don't just show up for everybody to use. Those who get them are being groomed for the highest ranks in the company. A coach also might be there to fix your one unacceptable flaw. If you can't be fixed, you will be toast. Either way, if you are offered an executive coach, you have just been offered gold.

Fatal flaws come in all sizes. Otherwise spectacular executives fail on the last rung of the ladder to the top because they just cannot eliminate their one fatal flaw. You can recognize colleagues with fatal flaws:

- They stab their boss in the back (usually only once).

- They are poor communicators.

- They are not aware of or do not care about the impact they have on others.

- They are not good role models.

- They have some key relationships that are broken and that they have been unable to repair.

So here they are, otherwise successful executives of sizable talent and worth, peering over the top of the ladder and eager to take that last step to the ultimate realization of their grand goal. But one thing stands in their way: their own behavior. The CEO gives such a person a strong signal, saying, "Here's a very expensive coach that I would like you to work with to prepare you for the future." And, often as not, the executive misses that signal. It's like running a red light at full speed during rush hour, except that instead of wrecking a car, the executive wrecks his or her career.

Learn to watch for the signals all along the way. Have a coach alongside you to spot the ones you miss. These signals will help you know if you're going up, down or sideways. They let you know the direction while there is still time to change it if need be.

"Life is a progress and not a station."
—Ralph Waldo Emerson

PART FOUR

DELIVER IMPRESSIVE RESULTS

SIX SECRETS FOR SUCCESS IN ANY BUSINESS

You now have some insights that will get you off to a great start in your career and help you develop lots of options that will lead you to success. You also have the tools to help you through the ups and downs of a courageous career. Your competition has been left at the starting line, trying to figure things out on their own. You've built an early lead.

Here comes the big however.

However, all the strategies and plans in the world won't help you one bit if you can't deliver in the workplace. You must perform, and perform better than the rest. This part of the book is designed to help you do just that.

No matter where you work or what you do, certain business facts and practices are absolutely critical to doing your job successfully. The six secrets we will explore are good everywhere, at anytime and for any business. Master these and you will always be ahead of the competition.

It takes decades to master the six secrets that we will explore. In fact, it takes most people a decade or longer to even know that they are important. Quite honestly, I don't think many people ever come to understand the power of the information what follows. You will, and that knowledge will distinguish you from your coworkers.

Let's have a look.

CHAPTER NINETEEN

SECRET NUMBER ONE: THE 80/20 RULE

*"Facts are meaningless. You could use facts to
prove anything that is even remotely true."*
—Homer Simpson

I guess it's not entirely honest to call something a secret when it has a principle in place to describe it and a book written about it. The principle is called Pareto's Principle. The book is *The 80/20 Principle* by Richard Koch.

SIMPLE BUT POWERFUL

The principle states that, in many events, roughly 80 percent of the effects come from 20 percent of the causes. A classic example involves the world's income distribution. About 80 percent of the world's income goes to about 20 percent of the people.

Still, I call the 80/20 Rule a secret because it seems that lots of people didn't learn about it in school or have forgotten about it. Yet it's one of the most powerful pieces of knowledge you can have when running a business. Perhaps it just sounds too simple.

Pareto had another theory that said, in part, people are often not motivated by logic and reason but rather by sentiment. Pareto, my main man, I think you are spot-on once again.

I already have immodestly managed to work in the fact that I had the good fortune to attend Harvard University. I may have shuffled right past the fact that it was only for three weeks. But those three weeks were three of the best learning weeks of my life.

We had a class of 144 people. We were all senior business leaders. Half were from the United States; the others were from the rest of the world. We worked in teams, worked almost exclusively on case studies, and presented our findings to everyone in one of those steeply tiered classrooms that I had always associated with law school (the closest I ever came to law school was watching *The Paper Chase* on TV).

Each day we had different business professors, some of the finest minds in the world. Each day for the entire three weeks, we were told that the dean of Harvard Business School would join us. Each day he had to cancel because he had to take a call from the president of the United States or make an emergency trip to Saudi Arabia or something else equally impressive.

On the last day of class, the dean made his appearance. His introduction took about fifteen minutes as the professor in charge of the program listed his various degrees, notable engagements and the books he had written. He came onto the stage to warm applause. We all wanted to hear from this guy.

The dean had his glasses propped up high on his forehead. He had his sleeves rolled up. Under one arm he had a hundred slides he planned to show on the overhead projector (this being the days before PowerPoint). We settled in for a long last day in the classroom.

The dean put down his slides. He faced the audience. He looked up in the air for a bit and stood silently. Just before it got really uncomfortable, he said, "I can tell you everything I know about business in one sentence. The 80/20 Principle works."

At that, he grabbed his slides, pulled the glasses back down onto his nose, and exited stage left.

That was the end of my Harvard education. It was also the most important business lesson of my life.

GO FOR ONLY THE GOLD

I had figured out some of this 80/20 stuff out on my own. I once determined that most of the business that came my way was either unacceptable or unprofitable. I was spending long hours sifting through the gravel, looking for that rare piece of gold. Lots of sifting. Very little gold.

First, I found out what the gold was in the business that came my way. I did some research to learn exactly what kind of business made my company the largest and most consistent profits. It turned out that step vans (step vans are those big brown trucks that UPS uses) were the most profitable thing we insured. This was probably because they were large, slow and operated exclusively within a well-defined and limited area. I also found that not only were these trucks wonderfully profitable to insure due to their being involved in very few accidents, they were also easy for us to handle as we issued the paperwork for the insurance contracts, making my job a breeze. One last cool thing about step vans: I could easily explain to our agents what they look like so they could go find them for us to insure.

I rented a step van, loaded it with doughnuts, and drove it around to the offices of my agents. I told the agents, "Find potential customers who have lots of these step vans because we love to insure them." They did. The company made money. The agents made money. The customers got the coverage they needed. And I graduated from crap sorter to moneymaker. Life was good.

I know all of this sounds so easy. It's not easy, and I am not sure why. I think we humans like complex things. I think the idea of forsaking business that might come our way so that we can concentrate on just the highly profitable items is against human nature. Whatever the reason, businesspeople often fail to understand the power of 80/20.

But once you understand it and accept it, you can apply the 80/20 rule to:

- Customers

- Distributors

- Products

- Locations

- Suppliers

- Employees

- Processes

- The data your company captures

- Report generation

- Travel

- Relationships

- How you spend your time

- Your goals

I hear lots of lip service about "working smarter not harder." I've heard it for years at work and read it in lots of business writings. The problem is most of us don't know how to do that. You do it with the use of the 80/20 Rule. Give that most profitable or rewarding top 20 percent at least 80 percent of your efforts and resources.

Effective use of the 80/20 Rule requires knowing what makes up the 80 and the 20. That data may be hard to find. Winners at work find it.

DEALING WITH THE PROFITABLE PAIN

Another real-life example:

I was asked to visit each of our offices and install a uniform plan for how we would work with our distributors. At each office we discussed all the distributors that the people there worked with and made decisions about how we would interact with them in the upcoming quarter and year.

At one of our West Coast offices I followed the same routine as I had everywhere else. Eventually we got around to discussing a quite large and well-known distributor. I asked what we should do with this distributor in the months and year ahead. The room became very quiet. People moved around in their chairs nervously and shot glances at one another. Finally the guy who ran the office said, "I hate to say it, but I think we should quit working with them."

The mood in the room immediately brightened. People spoke up in support of their boss.

"These people are too demanding."

"They want us to treat them special."

"They are always asking for favors."

"They want us to spend way too much time with them."

The boss smiled sheepishly. He suspected I would not be very happy with his suggestion that we essentially fire a large and well-known distributor. He was wrong. I was horrified.

I asked the team if they were aware that this distributor was the single most profitable distributor in the history of our company. I asked them if they were prepared to give up 20 percent of their top line and 80 percent of their bottom line to end the distributor's demands on us? I calculated the profits generated from this distributor, applied it against the average salary and benefits of an employee in that office and asked if they had identified the twelve people they would need to let go as soon as we terminated the relationship. That last question seemed to get their full attention.

Of course the distributor wanted more attention. Of course they wanted to be treated special. They were the 20 in the 80/20.

After the near riot subsided, someone asked, "How will we ever find time to service them the way they demand?"

How indeed? The answer involved all the little and unprofitable relationships that filled their every waking moment. Eliminate the time wasters and apply the hours and resources you save to the relationships that can make you some money.

TOO MUCH INFORMATION

Here's another example:

I took over a job that operated in half of the country. We sold about a dozen products in each of the states in our territory. Each product and each state had a report. The day I moved into the new office, the paper reports started coming in (reports we would now get via the computer). I stacked each report neatly in the corner of my office. At the end of two months, I had to remove the ceiling tiles to make room for the stack. That was when I called our information guru and asked him to come visit me.

The monolith I had built did not amuse him. He told me that my predecessor had read every one of those reports. I suggested that he must not have understood his job. His job was to find the gold in that data, not to spend his day analyzing all things useless. We argued until lunch.

After lunch, I showed the information guru what I meant. I knocked down the monolith, rooted around in the mound of paper, and found the report for the automobile insurance we wrote in Montana. The report was an inch thick. We flipped through each page. When we finally got to the last page, I pointed at the bottom line. Our multibillion-dollar-a-year company had exactly $861 of commercial automobile insurance in the entire state of Montana.

Just because we could produce an inch of data on $861 worth of business didn't mean we needed to do so.

I told him that I needed to know the *outliers*. Where did we make most of our profits? Where did we have most of our losses? I told him that this data would drive our strategy and our actions. He turned out to be an exceptionally smart guy (I determined that as soon as he agreed with me) and redesigned the reports to help me do my job. This was using 80/20 to drive a report structure.

I'll bet I've made the sale on the 80/20 Rule. You may have been on board before you read these pages. What still concerns me is that I have never met anyone who doesn't understand the principle—in theory. Your competitive advantage will materialize only when you actually *put it into practice*. It is harder to do than you might think.

Secret number one—*The 80/20 Rule*—is worth all of the other secrets put together. Just like the dean from long ago said, "All I know is that the 80/20 Rule works."

"Complexity is not to be admired. It's to be avoided."
—Jack Trout

CHAPTER TWENTY

SECRET NUMBER TWO: STOP FIXING.

"There is nothing so useless as doing efficiently that which should not be done at all."
—Peter Drucker

This secret is closely related to the 80/20 Rule. It's the actions that need to result once you embrace that rule.

I spent my whole career around sales management. I made it my business to find out what made some people successful and caused others to fail. Was it their confidence? Their appearance? How hard they worked? The way they communicated with their sales staff? What was it?

The closest I came to figuring it out is that great sales managers don't waste their time on people who can't sell.

BUILD ON SUCCESS

Consider this example: two people take over sales territories. Each has ten sales people reporting to them. The two sales teams are nearly identical in their makeup.

One sales manager decides to devote his attention to the weakest three sales people. Those in the middle are going to hit their quotas, and those at the top will exceed theirs. The plan is to get each of the bottom three up to at least one dollar of sales above the very bottom of the acceptable level.

The second manager finds that her top two people are producing 80 percent of the sales in her unit. She speaks to them and learns that they think they could produce twice that amount of business if they had some backroom support. The second manager uses some of her budget and many of her own hours to provide that support.

Which of the two sales managers do you think will have the most sales this month? I will give you a hint: You know how I think. That's right, number two wins the month. It's not even close.

My theory is only a theory, but it's based on a career-long observation of sales management winners and losers. The winners don't have to be told "Stop fixing."

We humans love the challenge of taking something that's broken and trying to fix it. I spent many years of my career attempting to fix the unfixable. Many of the otherwise smartest people I know continue this practice to this day.

I think our desire to fix things comes from our egos. I know that I never met a challenge I didn't like. I sometimes think I can do anything. I have the scars and failures to prove those thought are mistaken.

If you find yourself spending your time trying to be a turnaround artist, you may be missing the point. *The point is to make money.* Show the world you know how to make money. Hard work can't be put in the bank. Money can.

KNOW WHEN TO FOLD 'EM

My most painful example of this phenomenon involved a profit center head who reported to me. I loved this guy (still do). However, his business had lost a lot of money. I told him we should shut it down. He wanted time to come up with an alternate plan. When he did come up with a plan, I told him it wasn't enough. At that point I all but told this guy the right answer: shut this puppy down now, save your best people and save yourself; we have other things we can do that are surefire moneymakers.

He would have none of it. He was going to finish what he started. He would find a way to fix it. He came up with more plans. And that was the end of that. I shut down the business.

If you stop fixing you can turn your attention to those parts of the business that are making money and that hold good promise of making even more money. Fixing things is like pushing a very heavy rock up a very steep hill. I find it much easier to push a successful rock down hill, running hard to keep up with it. Running is fun. Pushing? Not my favorite thing.

When you're first starting out in a career, you don't have the ability to just unilaterally stop fixing. In fact, you'll always need to stop fixing with the full approval and buy-in of your boss or team.

People who can size up a problem and quickly decide that

it's not worth fixing are valuable. And they're in short supply. If you can become known as someone who has the good sense to stop fixing things that shouldn't be fixed, you will succeed all that much faster.

"Every analysis of actual allocation of resources and efforts in business that I have ever seen or made showed clearly that the bulk of time, work, attention, and money first goes to problems rather than to opportunities, and, secondly, to areas where even extraordinarily successful performance will have minimal impact on results."
—Peter Drucker

CHAPTER TWENTY-ONE

SECRET NUMBER THREE: TRUST . . . BUT VERIFY.

"In God we trust, all others we virus scan."
—Author unknown

I first heard the phrase "Trust . . . but verify" from Ronald Reagan. He was talking about something fairly important: mutual nuclear disarmament between the old Soviet Union and us. At the signing of a treaty with the Soviet Union, President Reagan used the phrase, and his Soviet counterpart, Mikhail Gorbachev, responded, "You repeat this phrase every time we meet."

Mr. Reagan answered, "I like it."

I like it as well. You can use the phrase as guidance throughout your career.

Remember my disaster with the jewelry-selling dog groomer? Imagine how much better off I would have been had I thought to trust . . . but verify.

IN YOUR OWN BUSINESS AND BEYOND

As I read the *Wall Street Journal* this morning I couldn't help noticing that our whole world could benefit from Mr. Reagan's favorite phrase. This morning's edition featured stories about

- A trusted financial guru who had taken billions of dollars from investors and used that money to run what was basically a Ponzi scheme. That is billions with a *B*. Looks like he fooled some pretty high-profile people.

- A guy who was just honored as entrepreneur of the year for all of Denmark. He wasn't there to pick up the award. He was on the run, trying to avoid arrest. Seems his software company enjoyed a huge sales increase because the other companies he owned borrowed money so they could buy the software company's products. Those companies didn't need that software; they bought it just to boost sales. Oh, and he didn't really have a PhD, as he claimed he did.

- A correction concerning a story in yesterday's edition of the *Journal* about Bed, *Beth* & Beyond. I'll bet Beth wishes the editor had verified the spelling on that one.

- Ulysses S. Grant (who hadn't been in the news much lately) and how he was taken to the cleaners by an "all hat and no cattle fast talker" back in 1881. This is the same Ulysses S. Grant who had been a renowned general during the Civil War and then served as our country's president. He and his son lost their money and much of their reputation to their business partner, some yahoo by the name of Ferdinand Ward. President Grant could have used President Reagan's good advice.

So how do you turn this good advice into a business tool that you can use to advance ahead of the competition?

The best place to use *Trust . . . but verify* is in every single management job you'll ever have. I'll leave that for another day and another book. It suffices to say you never outgrow *Trust . . . but verify*.

But what about those who seek success outside of a management career? What about those of you reading this book years before you become a manager? How can you use it on day one?

Two ways: In your day-to-day work, and as a home run. Let's look at day-to-day first.

YOU'LL TAKE THE BLAME

One of the good and bad things about business is that your final product is not just your product. You'll do much of the work, but someone has to produce the paperwork, manufacture the product, and get it delivered on time. It's a team effort.

When the product or service is delivered to your customer, your name is on it. When that product is defective, your name is on it. When it is delivered to the wrong address on the wrong day, it has your name on it.

You can't check every item that goes out with your name on it. But you *can* check enough units to make sure that everything is on track. You *can* check the final product or service that's being sent to your best customer. In fact, this might be a good place to combine the 80/20 Rule with your need to verify. Make sure you verify the very important work outputs—with your own eyes.

Some of the biggest workplace mistakes—and the biggest career derailments—happen because someone supporting someone else didn't do his or her job correctly. And when it all blows up, the person who was not given the proper support gets all the blame. Clients don't care one bit about the inner workings of your company. If you own the relationship, you are the company.

To me, this always seemed to be *the* unfair part of work. Someone else screws up, and you get the blame. Unfair? Yup. But it is what it is. If the final product is going to be delivered to your best customer or to your boss with your name on it, it's time to trust . . . but verify.

Here are the things I've heard people say as their careers, at least temporarily, plummeted over the cliff because someone else screwed up: "I trusted her to do her job." "I'm too busy to do everyone else's job for them." "I assumed it would be done right." "I normally let my customers do the final quality check. If there are mistakes, they find them, and I get them fixed. Who knew that this [new and really important] customer was used to having someone do that work for them?"

Think of my poor buddy with the decimal problem. Had

he taken a moment to have someone verify his math, he would have missed the most embarrassing moment of his career.

Trust . . . but verify. It will serve you well every day. Let your competition learn the lesson the hard way. You don't have to.

SWING AWAY OR CHECK

Regarding the home run, there's a business adage that warns against always trying to hit the homerun at work. It basically says that it's your job to get on base—get a walk, hit a single, win a little bit at a time. It warns that those who are always swinging for the fences often miss.

I agree with the adage. But most careers go along at a deliberate pace. Most people advance rather slowly and then hit a plateau at some point. The top 5 percent advance fairly slowly but never stop advancing. A fortunate and unusually talented few advance quickly. And then there's the odd situation, the person who advances at a normal pace and then has a major-league breakthrough. That breakthrough is usually because of a home run.

A breakthrough can take various forms:

- Someone advances two levels at once.

- The thirty-five-year-old in the cubicle next to you is sent to the home office to work directly for the president of the company.

- One of your teammates is made team leader of a very important new team.

On rare occasions, these breakthroughs happen because the person remembers to trust . . . but verify, while everyone else, including his or her boss, was "doing their job."

I've seen this happen a number of times in my career.

TOO GOOD SHOULD BE A TRIGGER

One time, our business in a very large city was losing money by large bucketfuls. We checked our work over and over and couldn't find the problem. Someone finally had the idea to verify the work of a vendor—work we had outsourced to the vendor because it had a reputation for excellence. We verified and found the problem. The vendor had hired a new person and didn't train or audit his work. His risk assessments were incorrect, and we had based our pricing on that misinformation, causing us to nearly go broke.

The person who thought to trust . . . but verify the vendor known for excellence made quite a name for himself. He had a career breakthrough shortly after the problem was corrected.

You know the old saying that "If it is too good to be true, it probably is"? Something that seems too good to be true should always trigger your trust . . . but verify instinct. It could lead to a home run.

We had someone take over a department that was plagued with a backlog of service requests. This was a problem that had gone on for a very long time. The new guy came in, and the problem disappeared almost over night. It was time to trust . . . but verify.

I'm not sure that I hit a homerun with my verification on

this one, but I did hit at least a double and got noticed by management for the very first time. I spoke up in a meeting, telling my boss that I didn't believe the reports, that I was receiving lots of calls that strongly indicated a service backlog still existed. I also mentioned that I had been working late and noticed that the new guy always took a box of papers with him when he left. My boss checked it out himself and found that the new guy's car trunk was loaded with service requests. He was taking them home each night and throwing them in the trash. It was an efficient and innovative strategy, but not a very effective one. The boss canned him and from then on he checked the backlog reports with his own eyes.

You need to save the boss or the big boss from making a huge mistake only once to get noticed. You can't live your life looking for these opportunities, but you can always be on the lookout for anything that's too good to be true.

GOTCHA EVENTUALLY COULD GET YOU

Let me add one more word on the responsible use of this powerful tool. Often you feel satisfaction when a competitor bites the dust. I can't say I was displeased when the hotshot who came in and got all the glory for cleaning up the backlog was discovered as a fraud. The Germans have a phrase for this feeling, *Schadenfreude*. It refers to the joy you derive from the misfortune of others. Gee, when you put it that way, it doesn't sound very nice.

However, we cannot let our teammates fail, even if that failure might move us up a peg.

A crook is not a competitor. A crook is a crook. I have very little sympathy for the backlog guy. I have zero remorse for helping to expose him.

But if I can help a teammate avoid a mistake that would harm the team, I always will offer my assistance. We stand for each other's success.

To trust . . . but verify gives you a competitive advantage. Use this tool wisely. Those who play "gotcha" die by a "gotcha."

> *"Trust everybody, but always cut the cards."*
> —Finley Peter Dunne

CHAPTER TWENTY-TWO

SECRET NUMBER FOUR: YOUR DATA IS GOLD.

"If you don't have a competitive advantage, don't compete."
—Jack Welch

We already explored why you need a competitive advantage at work. Without such an advantage you'll have to wait for the tide to come in and lift everyone's boat at once. And if your advantage is not something sustainable, someone will come along and copy or improve on what makes you special. A sustainable competitive advantage is completely golden and hard to come by.

Like people, companies need a sustainable competitive advantage. Some have it.

- The Parker Brothers company had it because it owned the patent on the game Monopoly. I say "had it," because the patent ran its course. And didn't it kind of make you mad that this company had a monopoly on Monopoly?

- The Treasury has it because it has a monopoly on

printing money.

• Walmart seems to have it because it's huge, it's everywhere, and it sells what people need inexpensively. It will be hard to out-Walmart Walmart.

The truth is most companies exist on competitive advantages, not sustainable competitive advantages. That's why it's so important that companies innovate or occasionally reinvent themselves.

Why is any of this important to you?

INFORMATION HAS ITS ADVANTAGES

Companies gather data that's theirs and theirs alone. If you recognize the importance of that data, know how to access and use it, and know what to look for, you can be the one who finds the sustainable competitive advantage. Why is it sustainable? Because only your company has access to this data.

For years, Allstate insurance was owned by Sears. Sears had data on something like 25 million households. Sears-owned companies such as Allstate had access to that data. No one outside of the Sears family could know what Sears knew. That data gave Sears and its companies a sustainable competitive advantage.

What gems are buried in the data that your company owns? What data do you have that can give you a personal or business advantage? If you ignore the data because "Data is not my job," you'll lose out on an outstanding opportunity to become highly valuable to your company.

The point here is always be looking. Like a hunter who

scans a wide field, hoping to spot the one object that's moving, look for the outliers. What can you find that's interesting?

CONSIDER THE UNCONVENTIONAL WISDOM

Counterintuitive is pretty cool. Counterintuitive says that the truth is sometimes the polar opposite of what your intuition tells you it is.

I know an insurance company that operated with the conventional wisdom that old drivers are lousy drivers. That wisdom makes sense. I know my eyesight and reflexes are not what they once were. Here's the problem: a careful review of data—data that only that company had—revealed that older drivers represented *the* most profitable part of their business. Armed with this data, the company went after older drivers, the drivers no one else wanted to insure.

A review of your own data will create pricing opportunities, suggest marketing campaigns, and help you see opportunities that no one else can see. It is a wonderful thing.

I always worked hard to learn things about my own part of the business that others couldn't learn. Earlier I mentioned my step van finding. That's a pretty good example. I found others along the way. For example:

- Businesses that required safety improvements when inspected had more losses than those that needed no improvements, even if those improvements were agreed to and completed.

- Swimming pools without fences had no more losses than swimming pools with fences. (Don't take that one to the bank, because that data is decades old. It was, however, quite true at one time and gave us a counterintuitive advantage in the marketplace.)

- Certain types of businesses in my area were processed quicker and more accurately than others. This increased customer satisfaction and decreased costs.

I know companies that found sustainable competitive advantage in some very odd data. They discovered that:

- Business generated from ads on one radio station was much more profitable than business generated from ads on another station.

- People with low credit scores had more losses than people with high credit scores. (Because of privacy issues, use of that data generated lots of controversy.)

- Cars with bumper stickers have more losses than those without bumper stickers. (Again, don't take that one to the bank. It was only one study. I never did trust that data, and it's as old as I am. Still, it's a pretty interesting fact, if it is true.)

I believe that all winners at work will derive some of their success—and perhaps much of their success—from their skillful use of the data they control. Learn to love the data.

DIG DEEP AND KEEP ONLY WHAT YOU NEED

Two side thoughts before we move along:

If you find that your department is gathering data that's

not required by some law or agreement and never helps you make more money, do what you can to stops its collection. Sometimes just knowing what data collection to kill will make you a very valuable person.

Next, just because your company doesn't collect data doesn't mean you can't find out things about your business that others don't know. The most valuable insights I ever got came from a manual review of my business. We looked in files. We gathered our own data. And we found some trends and facts that no one else could know. Sounds old-fashioned. It's not; this kind of research was never in fashion. However, you and your team can do it, and it might just pay some huge dividends.

> *"Here is a philosophy of boldness to take advantage of every tiny opening toward victory."*
> —Arnold Palmer

CHAPTER TWENTY-THREE

SECRET NUMBER FIVE: FOCUS . . . ON THE MONEY.

*"The ability to focus on important things is
a defining characteristic of intelligence."*
—Robert J. Shiller

What does Corporate America honor? It honors the making of money—or at least that's what it claims. Yet, what do we see in the workplace? Lots of moving parts that produce nothing that will add a nickel to the bottom line. We see activity without productivity—hard work, but no hard cash.

Do you want to stand out from the crowd? Then do what the most successful business owners learned to do long ago. Put your focus on those things that make the company money.

WORK HARD, BUT WORK SMART

Most of the high-potential and high-achieving people I know are extremely busy. I've seen busyness derail more than a few hardworking but misdirected people. Getting noticed at work is not about working hard; it's about making money.

If you have more work to do than you can complete, focus on the money. Do the moneymaking actions first. Book the business. Call on the client who has provided you the most profit. Correct the accounting error that will immediately add profit to your bottom line. Focus on the money.

I worked with a great guy who was focused on everything but the money. We worked in Southern California, in a place where you could throw a rope out the window and have it land on more potential business than most states had within their entire borders.

Every year this teammate of mine headed up to Wyoming for a rodeo thrown by one of our distributors. One year he invited me to join him. I checked out how much business we had in Wyoming—less than $10,000. Our profit margin on that business was about 5 percent. Flying up there would cost us considerably more than the $500 profit we made from the state. I told him I couldn't go and that he shouldn't go either. Talk about not being focused on the money!

MAKE TIME FOR THE MONEYMAKERS

I don't know anyone who doesn't want to complete everything assigned to him or her. However, I do know people who would be better off if they didn't complete all their assignments. Let's just call those people everybody.

When you start out in business you don't have the where-withal to unilaterally refuse or neglect to do something that has been assigned to you. You do have the ability to figure out what you will do first and last. You do have the ability to negotiate deadlines. You do have the ability to question if and how an activity will contribute to the profitability of the firm. You also need to have the smarts to know when to quit questioning and do the work assigned. Some days will be like that.

The closer I got to the top of an organization the more I saw people focusing on the big-money items. In fact, sometimes it was kind of embarrassing. For example, I would hear an executive kick off some required training program, and then I would hear him say he wouldn't be attending the training because he was working on a big-money deal. He was being a bit disingenuous perhaps, but he was right on the money.

Throughout your career you constantly will be deciding how to use your time. If you learn which of your activities makes the most money for the company and then do mostly that activity, you will increase your value and be on the road to becoming that person all of Corporate America prizes, the moneymaker.

"Show me the money."
—Jerry Maguire

CHAPTER TWENTY-FOUR

SECRET NUMBER SIX: THE MOST IMPORTANT WORD IN BUSINESS IS *CUSTOMER*.

*"Be everywhere, do everything, and never
fail to astonish the customer."*
—Attributed to Macy's department store

There are thousands of different jobs out there. Some put the employee in direct contact with the customer. Others are inside the office walls, with no customer contact. No one job is more important than another. However, the customer is more important than any of us.

Regardless of what your job is, find a way to be in regular contact with your company's customers, and you will improve your ability to make money.

MEET YOUR CUSTOMERS—IN PERSON

I know people who have been in business for forty years and have never met a customer. *Never.* And yet they make decisions that affect the customer. I believe that it is impossible to understand you customers by proxy.

Allstate had a great research facility. The company knew how to conduct customer research; collected data that validated that research; spent money to understand the wants, needs and requirements of customers; and put company people in front of those customers so they could improve their understanding of how their customs think. I had the great privilege of attending dozens of focus group meetings and many other events that featured real, live customers. They were among the most enlightening experiences of my life.

If you have a chance to listen to them, customers will tell you what they want, need and expect from a company. I would listen to their requests and weeks later end up in a room of executives who would then tell me what the customer really meant. Often, these executives had never met a customer. The executives were basically telling us what we had to sell, not what the customer needed or desired. Your company also could be ignoring its customers.

LISTEN, DON'T INTERPRET

At one place I worked, we started taking videos of our customers talking in a focus group setting. We would play the video and hear customers say that they wanted low prices. In one memorable piece of video, the customer looked around to find the camera, walked over to it, and said, "Whoever is listening to this on video tape, I want to make something crystal clear. I have one requirement for your product and one requirement only. I want a low price. Is that clear? I care about price, and I want you to get it as low as possible. That is all I want from you."

As soon as the room lights went on, one of the executives who had just watched that video said, "Let me tell you what he really meant by that. What he meant was he wants great service and a low price. I think what he said is a little misleading."

Oh my. The customer was not misleading at all. I think people who have never met customers sometimes think they are stupid. People running their own businesses are not stupid. Blunt, yes. Demanding, often. Stupid, rarely.

THEY'RE ALL ABOUT THE CUSTOMER

These preceding few chapters—The 80/20 Rule, Stop fixing, Trust . . . but verify, Data is gold, and Focus . . . on the money—are all about the customer.

The 80/20 Rule: Know who your important customers are so you can give them the kind of products and services they need to continue their profitable relationship with your company.

Stop fixing: Quit wasting your time and energy on things that take focus away from your profitable customers. Use your scarce assets on them and them only.

Trust . . . but verify: Customers deserve to have their quality expectations met. You cannot guarantee good quality unless someone, maybe even you, verifies that work.

Data is gold: Data can tell you things about customers that they may not know about themselves. If you can use your data to help them improve their own business, that's fantastic. No one else can provide that service.

Focus . . . on the money: Spend your time on profitable customers and not on distractions.

It is all about the customer. The sooner you come to understanding that, the sooner you'll be on the road to true success.

You may have to ask to find a way to get connected to your company's customers. You may be told to just do the work in front of you. No problem. Do the work and keep asking. You'll get your chance, and you will come to understand that the customer connection is the most important thing in this book. Make the connection, and you are golden.

"Sham Harga had run a successful eatery for many years by always smiling, never extending credit, and realizing that most of his customers wanted meals properly balanced between the four food groups: sugar, starch, grease, and burnt crunchy bits."
—Terry Pratchett

AND IN CONCLUSION . . .

I envy you.

You are just starting or restarting a journey that will take you where you want to go. It will require all your wit, wisdom, energy and resolve to make it to your destination. You won't have to wait to get to your destination to find enjoyment and satisfaction. You will find it all along the way.

You can do this. It's within you. You don't have to be special to get it done. But getting it done will make you special.

Ethics and fair play will be important on your journey. If you live your life in a way that says, "I'm honest, and I will treat you fairly," you will make it easy for others to partner and do business with you. You can play hard—in fact, you can play hardball—and still be completely honest and fair. Winning by cheating ain't winning. It's cheating. It is beneath you.

Expect some business and personal failures along the way. Know that you will get tired from time to time, become discouraged, and want to settle. We all do. Those of us who end up winning find a way to make it through. If you lose the path, find a new one.

At the end of your career, even if you have not taken over the whole known universe, declare yourself a success and move on to the next phase of your life. You will still be a valuable person. Your value in the bigger world is not dependent on your value at work. You will always be valuable no matter what. In fact, you are valuable at this very moment.

I mention this again because it's easy to forget our value. It's also easy to forget that the person in the mailroom, the janitor, your driver or the waiter who is serving you at dinner is an equally valuable person. Treat these people as you would want to be treated. Treat them that way on your first day on the job and on the day you are named king or queen. If you do, everything will all end up just fine.

Happiness can be found in the journey. And the one thing I really wish for you is happiness. May your happiness be abundant and may your smile be your lifelong companion.

Respectfully,

Donald J. Hurzeler

REFERENCES

I love quotes, as you can tell from reading this book. My house is filled with books of quotes, scraps of paper with quotes jotted on them, and quotes that friends have e-mailed to me.

QUOTATIONS

My thanks go to the following people who have provided me with quotes over the years:

Mark Roso, a colleague and friend from my Zurich Financial Services days. Mark provided a number of his followers with quotes every morning. Here's one of my favorites that Mark sent to me. It's by George Bernard Shaw: "*This is the true joy in life. Being used for a purpose recognized by yourself as a mighty one. Being thoroughly worn out before you are thrown on the scrap heap. Being a force of nature instead of a feverish selfish little clod of ailments and grievances complaining that the world will not devote itself to making you happy.*"

Marc Nuessen, a past student, a colleague, and a friend from my insurance days. Marc continues to provide me with the occasional spot-on quote. Here's one from an unknown author that I took as a personal lesson:

"There are four things you can never recover:

The stone after it is thrown.

The word after it is said.

The occasion after it is lost.

The time after it is gone."

Robert Gorman, my longtime writing coach and one of the best business writers and thinkers that I have ever met. Bob's e-mails are so good that I included a quote from one of them in the book.

I am grateful to the following websites that I used to find the rest of the quotes for this book. They include Wisdomquotes.com, BrainyQuotes.com, Focusdep.com, Quotegarden. com, ThinkExist.com, Wow4u.com, Gala.com, About.com, Happyworker.com, Resilienceproject.com, Personal-development.com, CheckZ.com, Quotationpage.com, Quotecosmos. com and Finestquotes.com. Where I just list the name of the author of a quote, you can be sure I found it on one of the websites listed.

Introduction
Belva Davis, from the *Women's Book of Positive Quotes* (Fairview Press, 2002)

Chapter One
Benjamin Franklin, from *Quotations of Benjamin Franklin* (Applewood Books, 2003)

Rick Nelson, "Garden Party," 1972.

Robert Gorman, from an e-mail to me dated December 5, 2008.

Napoleon Bonaparte, from *The Book of Positive Quotes* (Gramercy Books, 1993)

Chapter Two

Henry Ford from *Quality Service Teamwork and the Quest for Excellence* (Successories Publishing, 1992)

Tupac Shakur, "Life Goes On," 1996

William J. Bennett from *The Book of Virtues* (Simon and Schuster, 1993)

Chapter Three

The Beatles, "Do You Want to Know a Secret?," 1963.

Rod Steward album *Spanner in the Works*, 1995

Robert Kennedy/George Bernard Shaw . . . first written by Mr. Shaw in *Back to Methuselah*, 1921.

Dale Carnegie

Chapter Four

Sir Edmund Hillary

Allen H. Neuharth

Paul Tillich

John Wayne

Chapter Five

St. Augustine

Sydney J. Harris

Chapter Six
Unknown
Frank Lloyd Wright

Chapter Seven
Les Brown
Zig Ziglar
Charles C. Noble
Elbert Hubbard from *And I Quote* (Thomas Dunne Books, 2003)

Chapter Eight
Ara Parseghian
John Russell

Chapter Nine
Keith Ferrazzi
Edgar Watson Howe from *The Book of Positive Quotations* (Gramercy Books, 1993)
Keith Ferrazzi

Chapter Ten
Henry Miller
W. Edward Deming
Unknown

Chapter Eleven
Henry Ford
Mignon McLaughlin

Chapter Twelve
Peter McWilliams
Confucius
Tim McMahon

Chapter Thirteen

Dennis Whorley

Helen Keller from *The Book of Positive Quotations* (Gramercy Books, 1993)

Abraham Lincoln from the *Yale Book of Quotations* (Yale University Press, 2006)

Chapter Fourteen

Peter Drucker

Unknown

Chapter Fifteen

Sophia Loren

Chapter Sixteen

Donald Trump from the television show *The Apprentice*, 2009

Donald Trump from the television show *The Apprentice*, 2009

Chapter Seventeen

Napoleon Hill

Elisabeth Kübler-Ross

Chapter Eighteen

Eric Kurjan from the April 12, 2009 *Toledo Free Press*

Paul Wellstone

Ralph Waldo Emerson

Chapter Nineteen

Homer Simpson from a column I read on ClickZ.com. The column was by Bryan Eisenberg, dated November 21, 2008, and he quoted Homer Simpson from the television show *The Simpsons*.

Jack Trout from *The Power of Simplicity* (McGraw-Hill, 1999)

Chapter Twenty
Peter Drucker
Peter Drucker

Chapter Twenty-one
Jack Welsh
Arnold Palmer

Chapter Twenty-two
Unknown
Finley Peter Dunne from *And I Quote* (Thomas Dunne Books, 2003)

Chapter Twenty-three
Robert J. Shiller
Jerry Maguire (and other characters) from the movie *Jerry Maguire*

Chapter Twenty-four
Macy's
Terry Pratchett

OTHER RESOURCES

In Chapter Twenty-one I mention several items from the *Wall Street Journal*. They are from the December 17, 2008, edition.

The Bed, Beth & Beyond item is from the "Corrections and Amplifications" box on page A2.

The General Grant story is from a column in that issue by John Steele Gordon, which appeared on page A21 of my edition.

The Danish entrepreneur of the year story is on page A18.

The other stories of malfeasance or suspected malfeasance can be found throughout that edition and in almost any other edition of the *Wall Street Journal*.

I highly recommend that you read the *Wall Street Journal* every day.

BOOKS

I mentioned several books, and I want to call your attention to others.

Koch, Richard. *The 80/20 Rule: The Secret of Achieving More with Less* (Broadway Press, 1999). An excellent book on the 80/20 Principle.

Ferrazzi, Keith with Tahl Raz, *Never Eat Alone* (Currency-Doubleday, 2005). *The* book on networking.

Lucht, John. *The Rites of Passage at $100,000 to $1,000,000 plus* (The Viceroy Press, 2005). *The* book on executive job changing.

Langley, Monica. *Tearing Down the Walls* (Wall Steet Journal Books, 2003). This book lets you see what "resignation" looks like in the workplace.

Friedman, Thomas. *The World is Flat* (Farrar, Straus and Giroux, 2005). The story of how money flows in the world economy. A must-read for everyone.

Spencer, Johnson. *Who Moved My Cheese?* (G.P. Putnam's Sons, 1998). The best book ever written about "change."

Trout, Jack with Steve Rifkin. *The Power of Simplicity: A Management Guide to Cutting Through the Nonsense and Doing Things Right* (McGraw-Hill, 1998). The title tells the tale.

Stack, Jack. *The Great Game of Business: The Only Sensible*

Way to Run a Company (Currency/Doubleday, 1992). Shows the power of understanding the numbers that drive a company's success.

I also mentioned Dr. Loretta Malandro and Malanadro Communication Inc. Check out their website at Malandro. com. You also may wish to speak with her or her staff about high performance training for your team. She can be reached at 480-970-3200. Loretta has written several books including S*ay It Right the First Time* (McGraw-Hill, 2003) and *Fearless Leadership: How to Overcome Behavioral Blind Spots and Transform Your Organization* (McGraw-Hill). *Fearless Leadership* is the best book on changing behavior in the workplace that I have ever read.

By the way, Loretta is an excellent keynote speaker if you want someone with intelligence, huge passion, high energy, and a worthwhile message.

I mentioned also the DiBianca-Berkman Group. They took me through some intense and excellent leadership training many years ago. I am forever grateful for their training and assistance. I must also admit that I have not been in contact with the group in some time. The last information I had was they were in business in Flemington, New Jersey.

The George Lopez comedy routine about being named Team Leader, from his Oglio Records *Team Leader* album, is a classic. Listen to it and remember my story of the boiling crabs pulling the escaping crabs back into the pot. God bless George Lopez for grabbing success despite the obstacles.

As for the Internet quote sites, thank you for your research and organization. You have changed the way we can access the quoted wisdom of our fellow human beings.

I've put a lot of work into making sure that the quotes I use represent a wide range of views. I don't necessarily agree with the viewpoints or philosophies of the people quoted, but I respect their insight on the topic at hand. Jesse Jackson and I might disagree on a number of political issues, but he described America as I see it when he said:

"America is not like a blanket . . . one piece of unbroken cloth, the same color, the same texture, the same size. America is more like a quilt . . . many patches, many pieces, many colors, many sizes, all woven together and held together by a common thread."
—from *And I Quote* (Thomas Dunn Books, 2003)

INDEX

ACKNOWLEDGEMENTS

Having an editor who encourages you, tells you the truth about your writing, improves the content of what you write, and then cleans up the grammar and spelling of your draft, well, that person is a blessing. In my case, that person is Bob Gorman. Bob is my editor, writing partner, and friend. Thank you, Bob, for being an important part of my life—and for paying attention in all of your English classes.

The hardest part about writing a book is finding a publisher that is willing to look at your work, shares a common vision with you, and is willing to add you to its roster of authors. The search for that publisher can be long, hard, and absolutely demoralizing. In my case, I don't have a literary agent, so the quest for a publisher was entirely up to me.

Well, it turns out that the quest is not entirely up to me. My absolutely fabulous friends Kathy Murray, Dr. Dan Tomal, and Charlie Thalheimer each pitched in to help me find a great publishing company. I want them to know how much I appreciate their efforts, support, and friendship. Thank you. Friends and networking—a powerful combination that gets results.

In the end, a highly valued friend—who is an author, a business owner and has partnered with me on a significant business project in the past—Dr. Loretta Malandro, connected me to Greenleaf Book Group, and I found my publishing home. Loretta, thank you, from the bottom of my heart. I hope your new book, *Fearless Leadership*, sells a million copies.

And now a moment about the good folks at Greenleaf Book Group. Admittedly, my exposure to the big-time world of book publishing is relatively limited at this point in my writing career. That is not to say I have not had multiple encounters with literary agents and publishing companies. Over the course of my two books, I've had a lot of contact with agents and publishers. They all seem buried in submissions, overwhelmed with inquiries, and unwilling or unable to take on another author. And then I came in contact with Clint Greenleaf III.

I don't want to set up Clint for unrealistic expectations from other potential authors, but my first message to him was answered—by him, within about two minutes. Within ten minutes I had all sorts of useful information about his firm and its process for submissions. From then on I dealt with real, live, and responsive people at Greenleaf. They reviewed my submission in record time, gave me straightforward feedback, and worked with me to design a publishing deal that worked for both of us.

I told Clint that in a publishing world that feels like molasses, Greenleaf feels more like Red Bull. The people there give me a positive jolt every time I come into contact with them.

So big thanks to Clint Greenleaf III, founder, chairman and CEO of Greenleaf Book Group; Justin Branch, the senior consultant on the project; Chris McRay, the production manager; Katelynn Knutson, the marketing associate; Brian Phillips, the graphic designer who put together the cover design; Heather Jones, the editorial assistant who worked with me on the final details of the manuscript; and the entire staff at Greenleaf. I am proud to be on the roster. Thanks for doing a great job.

And who knew how much work went into the proofreading of a book? I certainly did not, but I know now. A giant Thank You to Larry Bean for his extremely detailed review of my manuscript. He has taught me a lot and now I wish I had paid better attention in school (he obviously did).

Jim Summaria has been taking professional pictures of me for thirty years. He managed to make me look presentable for my picture on the cover flap. That is not an easy job these days and I am most appreciative.

My appreciation also to David Ratner and his team at Newman Communications. David is my publicist. Thanks, David, for getting the word out for me.

And if you, dear reader, have managed to read this book all the way to the end of the Acknowledgements, I want to thank you as well. Not much point in writing a book if people do not read it. Thanks for making this exercise all worthwhile.

Drop me an e-mail at don.hurzeler@mac.com if you want to comment on the book, make suggestions for improvements for future editions, or just to get in contact with me. I am a little like Clint Greenleaf; I will be back to you quickly, if I am anywhere near e-mail access. I appreciate my readers. Thanks for spending this time with me.

ABOUT THE AUTHOR

Donald J. Hurzeler, CPCU, CLU, was born and raised in Southern California. He and his wife, Linda, have lived all over the United States and currently reside in the Chicago suburbs. They are in the process of moving to Kailua-Kona, Hawaii—the Big Island.

Over a forty-year corporate career, Don held jobs that put him in charge of training, communications, marketing ,and underwriting. He was a department head, branch manager, chief sales officer, and chief marketing officer. He served as chief underwriting officer for Zurich U.S. Don was also the CEO and president of Zurich Middle Markets, a billion-dollar part of the Zurich Financial Services organization. Don was president of the Zurich Foundation, president of a local United Way, national president of the 25,000-member Society of Chartered Property and Casualty Underwriters, and a member of the board of directors of American Nuclear Insurers.

Don loves to write and has been a writer throughout his life. He was a columnist for the Barrington (Illinois) *Courier* and for various insurance-related publications, including *Best's*

Review. His first book, *Designated for Success*, was published in 2004.

As a speechwriter, Don wrote speeches for executives at both Allstate insurance and Zurich Financial Services. As a speaker, he has done extensive public speaking, including keynote addresses to business groups and university students in the United States and in Europe.

Don was the 2005 Golden Torch Award honoree for leadership and innovation within insurance communication, an honor bestowed by the Insurance Marketing Communications Association (IMCA).

A 1969 NCAA Division II Track and Field All American, Don is a member of the Chapman University Athletic Hall of Fame. He is a self-described "middle of the pack" marathon runner who has run both the Pikes Peak Marathon and a marathon inside a cave in Holland.

Don has been married for more than forty years to Linda. They have a son, Jim Hurzeler, and a daughter, Stephanie Stanczak, and two grandchildren, Ava and Nathan Stanczak. Don is retired from corporate life and will continue to write and speak on various business topics, including career- and insurance-related topics. He is also a photographer and has posted his photos at http://gallery.me.com/don.hurzeler.

Don can be reached at don.hurzeler@mac.com. Don's website is www.donhurzeler.com.